Let's Get Fruity

WRITTEN BY
ANNIE VAFIADIS & JANE CLIVE

PUBLISHED BY HEATH & WILLINGSWORTH PUBLICATIONS

Designed and Printed by Aspect Design, 89 Newtown Road, Malvern, Worcs. WR14 2PD

Let's Get Fruity

Soups, Starters and Snacks

Emma's Pear and Watercress Soup

(Serves 6)
1 bunch watercress
3 ripe comice pears, peeled sliced
1$^1/_2$ pt/900ml chicken stock
salt
freshly ground black pepper
6fl oz/175ml double cream
juice of half a lemon

Serve it hot when there's a nip in the air or cold on a balmy, early autumn day

1. Wash and pick over the watercress. Cut off the green leaves and reserve.
2. Place the watercress stalks and pears in a pan with the stock, add salt and pepper to taste.
3. Bring to the boil, cover and simmer gently for 15 minutes. Remove from the heat.
4. Process the soup in small batches with the watercress leaves in a processor or blender then sieve to remove debris.
5. Stir in the cream, lemon juice and extra salt & pepper if necessary. Serve hot or cold.

Winter Bramley Chowder

(Serves 4)
1 lb/450g smoked haddock
1 pt/600ml milk
$^1/_2$ pt/300ml water
2 oz/50g butter
1 large Bramley apple, peeled cored and cubed
$^3/_4$ oz/20g flour
6 oz/175g white potatoes, washed and diced
2 tbsp/30ml freshly chopped parsley
nutmeg
salt and freshly ground black pepper

1. Place the haddock, milk and water into a large saucepan, slowly bring to the boil, cover and simmer for 8-10 minutes until the fish is cooked and flakes easily.
2. Carefully remove the fish using a fish slice onto a plate and set to one side to cool.
3. Strain the cooking liquid and reserve.
4. Heat the butter in a saucepan and add the apples, fry until softened then stir in the flour. Add the reserved cooking liquid and potatoes, bring to the boil stirring all the time. Place a lid on the pan and simmer for 20 minutes or until the potatoes are tender.
5. With a fork skin flake and bone the cooked fish, add the fish to the chowder with the chopped parsley, season well with nutmeg, salt and pepper. Serve immediately.

Conference Soup
(Serves 6)

6 ripe Conference pears, peeled, cored and chopped
$^3/_4$ pt/450ml vegetable stock
6 tbsp/90ml lemon juice
6oz/175g Cheddar cheese grated
5fl oz/150ml single cream
1 tbsp/15ml finely chopped parsley
Salt and freshly ground black pepper`

1. Place the pears, lemon juice and stock into a saucepan and bring to the boil, reduce heat and simmer gently until the pears are tender, approximately 5 minutes.
2. Place in a blender and process until smooth, return to the saucepan.
3. Add the Cheddar, cream and parsley, and season. Stir soup over a low heat until the Cheddar has melted and the soup is heated through then serve.

Tomato, Apple and Celery soup
(Serves 4)

1pt/600ml chicken stock
4oz/100g onions chopped
6oz/175g tomatoes quartered
6oz/175g Fiesta apples quartered
6oz/175g celery cut into 2"/5cm lengths
2oz/50g butter
4 tbsps/60ml dry sherry
large pinch of salt
freshly ground black pepper
pinch of ground ginger
fresh chives to garnish

1. Melt the butter in a large, heavy based pan, add the onions and cook gently until golden.
2. Add to the pan the sherry, vegetables, apples, ginger and seasoning. Leave to sweat, simmer very gently for 1 hour stirring often to prevent sticking.
3. Add the stock and stir, continue cooking until vegetables are soft.
4. Divide into two batches and process until smooth, reheat, season and serve garnished with freshly snipped chives.

Celeriac and Bramley Soup
(Serves 4)

12oz/350g celeriac
2 medium sized Bramley apples
1oz/25g butter
1 large onion, thinly sliced
1¹/₂ pts/900ml vegetable stock
bouquet garni

To make a Bouquet Garni, use sage, thyme, chives, bay leaf and parsley tied in square of muslin

1. Chop the celeriac into small, thin pieces. Peel, quarter, core and slice the apples.
2. Melt the butter in a heavy based saucepan on a low heat and add the celeriac, apples and onion, cover and cook very gently for 10 minutes.
3. Pour in the stock and bring to the boil, add the bouquet garni, cover and simmer for 35 minutes.
4. Remove the bouquet garni and cool the soup slightly, divide into two batches and process until smooth, reheat and serve.

Parsnip and Apple Soup
(Serves 4)

1lb/450g parsnips
1 Falstaff apple
1 oz/25g butter
1 medium onion, chopped
2 pts/1200ml vegetable stock
¹/₄ pt/150ml single cream
salt & pepper
2 tbsp/30ml freshly chopped parsley

1. Melt the butter in a large saucepan. Saute parsnips apple and onion until soft.
2. Add the stock, bring to the boil, reduce heat and cover., simmer for approximately 45 minutes or until the vegetables are tender.
3. Allow to cool then liquidise. Add the parsley season and reheat. Add the cream just before serving.

Pear and Stilton Salad
(Serves 4)

Prepare just before serving

3oz/75g blue stilton
3oz/75g chopped walnuts
3 large ripe Concorde pears
1 tbsp/15ml lemon juice
4 tbsp/60ml cream sherry
lollo rosso lettuce

1. Crumble the stilton and mix with the walnuts, halve the pears lengthways, core and slice thinly.
2. Divide between 4 serving plates arranging neatly down the centre. Sprinkle with cheese mixture. Mix the lemon juice and sherry together and spoon over the pears. Garnish with some lollo rosso.

Howgate and Herring Salad
(Serves 2)

4oz/100g soused herrings, chopped
4oz/100g grated Howgate apple
1tbsp/15ml mayonnaise
seasoning

1. Mix together all the ingredients, chill and serve on a bed of lettuce.

Waldorf Salad
(serves 4)

Prepare just before serving

1 head of celery, washed and chopped
3 Cox apples, sliced
2 bananas, sliced
4oz/100g walnuts, chopped
salt and freshly ground black pepper • mayonnaise

1. Mix all the ingredients together apart from the mayonnaise, season with salt and pepper and serve with a seperate dish of mayonnaise.

Bumbles
(Serves 4)

4 large Falstaff apples
4 tbsp/60ml clear honey slightly warmed
4oz/100g wafer thin smoked ham chopped
4oz/100g cheddar cheese, sliced thinly

1. Pre-heat the grill and line the pan with foil.
2. Core peel and slice each apple into 4 rings, place into grill pan and using half of the warmed honey brush each ring before placing under the hot grill for approx 2 minutes.
3. Turn the apple rings over and brush on the remaining honey, mix the ham with the cheese and sprinkle over the rings, grill for a further 2 minutes.
4. Reform the rings into 4 apple shapes and serve with a little green salad.

Upton Rarebit
(Serves 2)

2 slices bread (white or brown, medium thick)
1oz/25g butter
1 small onion chopped
1 small Jonagored apple sliced and chopped
$^1/_2$ oz/15g flour
5fl oz/150ml brown ale
$^1/_2$ tsp/2.5ml mustard
$^1/_2$ tsp/2.5ml brown sauce
dash Worcester sauce
4oz/100g strong cheddar cheese grated
1 egg size 3 lightly beaten
salt • freshly ground black pepper
pinch cayenne pepper

1. Gently fry the onion and chopped apple in butter.
2. Stir in the flour, take off the heat and add the brown ale, bring to the boil and add the mustard, brown sauce, Worcester sauce and cheese — simmer for 2 minutes.
3. Remove from the heat and add the beaten egg, salt, pepper, cayenne; return and heat gently,
4. Meanwhile toast the bread, cover with rarebit mixture. Place under a pre heated grill until brown and bubbling.

For Upton Buck Rarebit omit the egg from cheese mixture, poach and put on the top.

Tasty Sandwich Treats
(Makes 2 rounds of sandwiches)

Gloucester Spread

2oz/50g Double Gloucester grated
2oz/50g Katy or Cox apple grated
1tbsp/15ml homemade chutney
1tbsp/15ml chopped spring onions

Cheddar Spread

2oz/50g Strong mature cheddar
grated
2oz/50g Elstar or Fiesta apple
grated
1tbsp/15ml homemade picalilli

1. For either sandwich, mix together all ingredients and season to taste.

Fruity Potato Fillers
(Makes enough filling for 2 medium sized baking potatoes)

Sausage Topper

2 medium sized pork sausages
cooked and sliced
1 stick of celery washed and sliced
2oz/50g Discovery or Ida Red apple
chopped
1 tbsp/15ml mayonnaise
1 tbsp/15ml thick natural yogurt
seasoning

Slimmers Dream

4oz/100g low fat cottage cheese
1oz/25g red pepper diced
2oz/50g Spartan apple chopped
1oz/25g sweetcorn
seasoning

*Mix all the ingredients together
and pile on top of baked potato*

Nutty but Nice

2oz/50g cooked chicken chopped
2oz Russett apple chopped
1oz/25g sultanas
1tbsp/15ml thick natural yogurt
1oz/25g walnuts chopped
seasoning

Festive Filler

2oz/50g cooked turkey chopped
2oz/50g Cox apple chopped
1tbsp/15ml cranberry sauce
seasoning

11

Bramley Fritatta
(Serves 4)

4 tbsp/60ml olive oil
1 garlic clove peeled and crushed
1 large potato, peeled and finely sliced
2 leeks, washed and finely shredded
1 Bramley apple, peeled and finely sliced
5 eggs, size 3
salt and black pepper
2oz/50g freshly grated Parmesan cheese
2oz/50g grated Edam cheese
1 tbsp/15ml chopped fresh basil

To skin garlic, select a clove and bang it with the flat side of a large knife, place your knife over the clove and hit it gently with your hand, the cracked clove will render itself skinless without effort.

1. Heat 3 tbsp/45ml of oil in a heavy based frying pan and saute the potatoes gently for 10 minutes or until tender. Remove from the pan and set to one side.
2. Heat the rest of the olive oil in the frying pan, add the leeks and apple slices, fry gently for 4 minutes until the apple and leeks soften, season well.
3. In a mixing bowl beat the eggs and season, stir in the potatoes, leek and apple then transfer to a frying pan, fry very gently for 10 minutes.
4. Pre heat the grill, sprinkle the cheeses and basil over the fritatta. Grill under a medium heat until the top is a golden brown and the fritatta is set (4-5 minutes).
5. Serve hot or warm cut into wedges with a fresh green salad.

Main Courses

Spicy Pear Stir-Fry
(Serves 4)

Always heat the pan before putting the oil in, so heat the pan, add the oil and the food immediately and the food won't stick.

2 tbsp/30ml olive oil
1 small onion, halved and thinly sliced
1 tsp/5ml ground cinnamon
2 tsp/10ml ground coriander
$1/_2$ tsp/2.5ml cayenne pepper • 1 tsp/5ml ground turmeric
1"/2.5cm piece fresh root ginger, finely chopped
1 lb/450g mixture of parsnips, swede, celeriac and potato, peeled
blanched and diced • 3 medium sized carrots, peeled and sliced
1 medium aubergine, halved and sliced
$1/_2$ bulb fennel, trimmed, halved and sliced
2 Conference pears, peeled cored and sliced
$1/_4$ pt/150ml vegetable stock • salt and freshly ground black pepper
4 tbsp/60 ml freshly chopped coriander

1. Heat the oil in a large heavy-based pan. Add the onion and cook until softened but not coloured.
2. Add the spices, and ginger, cook gently for 2 minutes, then add the remaining ingredients except the fresh coriander.
3. Stir-fry over a medium heat for 15-20 minutes, stirring. Season and stir in the freshly chopped coriander and serve at once with crusty bread and a fresh green salad.

Pork Guard of Honour with Scrumpy Apple Stuffing (serves 8-10)

4lb/1.75kg loin of pork in two pieces with 5 chops in each
6oz/175g onions, finely chopped
1oz/25g butter • 3oz/75g coarse white breadcrumbs
2 level tsps/10ml fresh or dried sage
1 large Bramley or 2 small Cox apples peeled, cored and chopped
5fl oz/150ml Dry Cider • freshly ground black pepper

1. Pre-heat oven to 375°F/190°C/mark 5
2. Wrap the trimmed bone ends in foil to prevent them burning and place the pork in a small roasting tin. Cook for approx $1^1/_2$ hours until the juices run clear.
3. Meanwhile melt the butter in a heavy based pan add the onions and cook for 3 mins add the apples and cook for a further 3 mins until the onions are transparent
4. Add all the other ingredients and bind together with the cider
5. Butter an ovenproof dish and place in the oven with the pork for the final $1/_2$ hour or until throughly cooked.

14

Pork with pear and hazelnut stuffing

(Serves 6)

6 loin pork chops, trimmed
1 tbsp/15ml oil
1 small onion, finely chopped
1 oz/25g hazelnuts, finely chopped
2 large Beurre Hardy pears, peeled, cored, finely diced
5 tbsp/75ml fresh wholemeal breadcrumbs
grated zest of 1 lemon
2 tbsp/30ml freshly chopped parsley
salt & freshly ground black pepper
$^1/_2$ egg, beaten
2 tbsp/30ml calvados or brandy
$^1/_2$ pt/300ml chicken stock
1 tsp/5ml cornflour blended with 1 tbsp cold water
Pear slices brushed with lemon juice, watercress sprigs

A ripe pear gives very slightly around the stem, but should in no way be squashy.

1. Heat the oil in a frying pan, add the onion and nuts and fry gently for 5 minutes until lightly golden. Pre-heat oven to 400°F/200oC/mark 6
2. To prepare the stuffing, mix together in a bowl the pears, breadcrumbs, lemon zest and parsley, season with salt and pepper.
2. Add the onion and nut mixture and stir well. Bind the mixture together with the beaten egg.
3. Arrange the chops in a greased roasting tin, place a spoonful of stuffing on top of each chop, and cover loosely with foil. Bake the chops for 50-60 minutes or until they are tender.
4. Transfer the chops to a heated serving dish and keep warm. Pour the brandy/calvados, stock and seasoning into a small pan, add the blended cornflour and water, bring to the boil stirring constantly until slightly thickened.
5. Serve the chops with a little sauce poured around. Garnish with the pear slices and watercress.

Severn Bore Pork
(Serves 4)

4 loin pork chops trimmed of excess fat
1oz/25g butter • 1tbsp/15ml olive oil
2 medium onions, peeled and sliced
1 garlic clove peeled and crushed
2 Crispin apples, peeled, cored, thickly sliced
$^1/_2$ tsp/2.5ml dried thyme
8 fl oz/250ml sweet cider • 1tbsp/15ml clear honey
1 tbsp/15ml brandy • salt and freshly ground black pepper
4 tbsp/60ml double cream

1. Pre heat oven 375° F/190° C/mark 5
2. Heat half the butter and the olive oil in a heavy based pan and fry the chops for 3 minutes on each side and transfer to a casserole.
3. Add the remaining butter to the pan and fry the garlic and onions for 3 minutes and add to the casserole.
4. Fry the apple slices for 1 minute on each side and add to the casserole together with the thyme, cider, honey and brandy. Season with salt and pepper and place in the oven for 35 minutes.
5. Remove the casserole from the oven and skim off any fat that has risen to the surface and stir in the cream before serving.

Spicy Bramley and Pork
(Serves 4)

1 medium sized Bramley apple, cored and sliced into 6 equal rings and halved
$1^1/_2$ lbs/675g Pork tenderloin, cubed • 1 oz/25g butter
1tbsp/15ml olive oil • 1 clove garlic, crushed
$^1/_2$ tsp/2.5ml ground coriander • $^1/_2$ tsp/2.5ml cumin
salt and freshly ground black pepper • 1 bunch spring onions, chopped
8 oz/225g button mushrooms, sliced
1 oz/25g toasted pinenuts
5 oz/125g natural yoghurt

1. Melt the butter and oil in a large heavy based pan add the garlic and cook for 2 minutes.
2. Place the sliced Bramley in the pan and turning occasionally, cook until soft and golden. Remove the apple slices and keep warm.
3. Stir in the coriander and cumin, add the pork and spring onions and fry until well cooked season to taste.
4. Add the mushrooms and cook for 1 minute.
5. Stir in the pinenuts and yoghurt.
6. Serve hot with the Bramley slices.

Gamekeepers Pheasant
(Serves 4)

1 brace of pheasants approx $1^{1}/_{2}$ lbs/700g each
8 rashers streaky bacon cut each in half length ways
Freshly ground black pepper
4 large Cox, Katy or Russett apples
1 small onion, chopped
3 oz/75g fresh breadcrumbs
2 oz/50g hazelnuts, chopped
2 tsps/10ml freshly chopped thyme
2 tsps/10ml freshly chopped sage
2 tsps/10ml freshly chopped marjoram
1 oz/25g butter

1. Preheat oven to 200°C/400°F/mark 6.
2. Wash and pat dry the pheasants, truss and cover each breast with the bacon and grind over a little black pepper.
3. Place the pheasants in a greased roasting tray and cover with foil. Roast for 40 minutes.
4. Core the apples and mix together the onion, breadcrumbs, nuts and herbs and use this mixture to stuff the apples.
5. Dot the apples with the butter, remove the foil from the roasting tin and place the apples around the pheasants, roast for a further 30 minutes or until the pheasants are cooked and their flesh is no longer pink.
6. Leave the pheasants to rest for 10 minutes before carving and make a thin gravy from $^{1}/_{4}$ — $^{1}/_{2}$ pt/150ml—300ml of hot meat stock, the juice from the pheasants and a little cornflour and cold water. Serve with game chips.

Duck Breast with Pears
(Serves 6)

6 Duck breasts
6 Firm Comice or Beurre Hardy pears - sliced
1 cinammon stick • 1 oz/25g butter
2 tbsp/30ml olive oil • 1 tbsp/15ml clear honey
2 medium onions, sliced and finely chopped
1 tbsp/15ml five spice powder
2 large ripe tomatoes
salt • freshly ground black pepper • a little sugar
2 tbsp/30ml sherry vinegar
$3^1/_2$ fl oz/112mls dry sherry
$^1/_2$ pt/300mls chicken stock

1. Pre-heat oven to 425°F/220°C/mark 7
2. Season the duck breasts with salt and pepper.
3. Put the pears and cinammon stick into a pan and add enough water to cover.
4. Bring to just below the boil and simmer until tender, strain and re-serve the cooking liquid.
5. Meanwhile heat the butter in a heavy based ovenproof pan over a medium heat and fry the duck breasts skin side down for approximately 8 minutes or until golden.
6. Drain off the fat and save, brush the skins with the honey and bake in the oven until tender approximately 15 minutes.
7. Meanwhile heat 2 tbsps/60ml of oil in a frying pan, add the pears and fry until golden, using a slotted spoon transfer to a plate and keep warm.
8. Add the onions and five spice powder to the frying pan along with the tomatoes and sugar and saute for 10 minutes until soft.
9. Pour on the sherry vinegar and continue to saute for 5 minutes.
10. Remove the duck from the oven and keep warm. Tip any fat into the onions and turn up the heat.
11. Add the sherry, stock and $^1/_2$ pt/300ml of the strained cooking liquid from the pears to the frying pan and bring to the boil uncovered for approximately 10 minutes to reduce it by about two thirds.
12. Process/liquidise the sauce return it to the frying pan and stir in any extra juices.
13. Arrange the duck with the pears on a plate and pour over the sauce, serve immediately.

Glazed Duck with Cherries
(Serves 4)

Cherries will stone easily if deep frozen

2 tbsp/30ml clear honey
2 tbsp/30ml dark soy sauce
4 duck breast fillets
1 tsp/5ml Dijon mustard
1 tbsp/15ml orange juice
3 tbsp/45ml walnut oil • 1 tsp/5ml red wine vinegar
350g/12oz dessert red cherries such as Stella, stoned
mixed salad leaves
2 tbsp/30ml chopped fresh chives

1. Preheat oven to 400° F/200° C/mark 6. Mix the honey and soy sauce brush over the duck and roast on a rack in the oven for 15-20 minutes until crisp but still pink inside.
2. Mix together the mustard, orange juice, oil and vinegar. Add the cherries, season to taste and toss thoroughly.
3. Slice the duck, arrange on a bed of salad leaves and spoon over the cherries and dressing. Garnish with the chives and serve with warm crusty bread.

Chicken and Apple Korma
(Serves 4)

In ancient Greece, garlic was seen as a symbol of strength and courage, it contains kyolic, a natural blood thinner - so eat plenty and do your heart a favour

2 tbsp/30ml olive oil
1 Greensleeves apple cored and thinly sliced
1 medium onion sliced
1 clove garlic crushed
1 tbsp/15ml ground coriander
1 tsp/5ml ground cumin
$^1/_2$ tsp/2.5ml ground turmeric
12 oz/350g lean chicken, cut into finger strips
4 oz/100g thick Greek yogurt • Salt and freshly ground black pepper
2 tbsp/30ml freshly chopped coriander • $^1/_4$ pt/150ml chicken stock

1. Heat two large frying pans and add 1tbsp/15ml of oil, apples and onions to one and fry until soft and brown.
2. Add the garlic and spices and fry for a further 2 minutes.
3. Put 1 tbsp of oil into the second pan and sauté the chicken strips over a high heat until sealed.
4. Add the chicken to the apple and onion pan, stir in the stock and simmer gently for 8-10 minutes then add the yogurt and seasoning. Serve immediately sprinkled with the chopped coriander.

Sage and Spartan Liver
(Serves 4)

Spartans are crisp and juicy apples with a refreshing perfumed flavour

1 lb/450g lamb's liver cut into strips
Seasoned flour
2 tbsp/30ml olive oil
1 medium onion, sliced
2 Spartan apples cored and cut into wedges
6 whole sage leaves
$^1/_2$ pt /300ml unsweetened apple juice • 2 tbsp/30ml tomato puree
2 tsp/10ml Dijon mustard • 4 tbsp/60ml fromage frais

1. Toss the liver in seasoned flour.
2. Heat a large heavy based frying pan add the oil and gently fry the onion until softened.
3. Push the onions to one side of the pan and add the liver and fry the strips for 2-3 minutes on each side.
4. Bruise the sage leaves and add these and the apples to the pan and fry for a further 5 minutes stirring occasionally.
5. Stir in the apple juice and tomato puree bring to the boil and simmer for approximately 5 minutes.
6. Stir in the mustard, fromage frais and seasoning and simmer gently for 1 minute before serving.

Berties' Bangers
(makes 12 fat sausages)

Never put garlic in the refrigerator - the peel will become moist and the head will dry out.

1 lb/450g lean minced pork
8 oz/225g pork sausagemeat
1 tsp/5ml hot chilli powder • 2 cloves garlic crushed
1 small onion finely chopped • 1 small Cox or Katy apple, grated
1oz/25g fresh breadcrumbs • 1 tbsp/15ml fresh parsley • 1 egg
6 rashers of smoked rindless bacon cut in half lengthwise
Salt and freshly ground black pepper

1. Mix the minced pork, sausagemeat, chilli powder, crushed garlic, onion, apple, breadcrumbs, parsley and seasoning together in a large bowl.
2. Beat in the egg until thoroughly combined and shape into 12 sausages and wrap in bacon. Cover and chill for at least 30 minutes.
3. Pre-heat the oven to 200°C/400°F/mark 6
4. Heat a large roasting tin and add the oil. Brown the sausages on all sides then transfer the tin to the oven and cook for approximately 45 minutes or until cooked thoroughly, drain on kitchen paper. Serve hot or cold

Braised Red Lamb
(Serves 4)

6oz/175g lamb mince
900g/2lb red cabbage, outer leaves and core removed, shredded
salt and freshly ground black pepper • 2 large onions finely chopped
2 large Bramley, Howgate or Grenadier apples peeled cored and finely
chopped • 2 cloves garlic finely minced
$^1/_2$tsp/2.5ml ground nutmeg • 3tbsp/45ml brown sugar
2oz/50g sultanas
3tbsp/45ml white wine vinegar or cider vinegar
25g/1oz butter

1. Preheat oven to 300°F/150°C/mark 2. Gently fry the lamb mince.
2. Mix together the onion, apple, garlic, nutmeg, sultanas and sugar.
3. Place a layer of shredded cabbage in an ovenproof dish, sprinkle with salt and pepper, then a layer of mince, and a layer of the apple and onion mixture. Repeat until all the ingredients are used.
4. Pour on the vinegar, dot with butter and cover the dish with a tight fitting lid or foil.
5. Place in the oven and cook slowly for 2 $^1/_2$ - 3 hrs.

Bramley Lamb
(Serves 4)

2 tbsp/30ml olive oil
2 lb/900g boned lamb shoulder/leg cut into 1" pieces
$^1/_2$ tsp/2.5ml English mustard powder • 1 large onion, sliced
1 small leek trimmed, rinsed, drained and sliced
1$^1/_2$ lb/675g Bramleys peeled cored and cut into chunks
3 cloves garlic crushed
$^1/_2$ pt/300ml red wine • $^1/_2$ pt/300ml vegetable stock
1 tsp/5ml fresh or dried thyme • 1 tsp/5ml dried oregano
Salt and freshly ground black pepper

1. Pre-heat oven to 375°C/190°F/mark 5
2. Heat a large heavy based frying pan add the oil and seal the lamb pieces quickly until lightly coloured and place in a casserole dish, sprinkle over the mustard powder.
3. Add the onion leek and apples to the frying pan and fry until just brown. Add the garlic, wine, stock and herbs. Season well, bring to the boil and pour over the lamb.
4. Bake for 1 hr 30 minutes or until the meat is cooked.

Gammon with Spiced Pears
(Serves 6)

Remember Gammon needs to be soaked before cooking

3lb-1.5kg piece of gammon
1 tbsp/15ml olive oil
1 onion, finely chopped
1 tsp/5ml plain flour
$^3/_4$ pt/450ml clear apple juice
$^1/_4$ pt/150ml dry white wine
1 cinnamon stick, halved
10 cloves
1 tsp/5ml black peppercorns
10 allspice berries
1 bay leaf
6 Glou Morceau pears, peeled with stalks left on
2 tbsp/30ml brandy
salt and pepper

1. Soak the gammon in cold water for 1-2 days, changing the water several times
2. Heat the oil in a flameproof casserole and fry the onion for 3 minutes until soft and golden, add the flour then stir in the apple juice and wine.
3. Drain the gammon and add to the casserole with the spices and bay leaf. Bring to the boil, reduce the heat, cover and simmer for $1^1/_2$ hours or until the gammon is tender
4. Add the whole pears and brandy and cook for 10-15 minutes until the pears are just tender, season to taste and serve.

Bacon Cheese and Apple Pie
(Serves 4)

PASTRY
12oz/350g plain flour
$2^1/_2$ oz/60g butter
$2^1/_2$ oz/60g lard
1 egg beaten
Pinch salt
Fat for greasing

10oz/300g freshly boiled potatoes
6oz/175g Rindless smoked or unsmoked streaky bacon
9oz/250g mature cheddar cheese
1-2 tbsp/ 15-30ml water
1lb/450g Bramley cooking apples, peeled.
1 small onion
salt & pepper
mixed herbs
milk for mixing
melted butter

1. Pre-heat oven to 350ºF/180ºC/Mark 4. Put the flour, fats and egg into a food processor and mix until blended, add cold water and mix to a soft dough.
2. Grease a loose bottomed $7^1/_2$ -8"/18-20cm cake tin 3"/7.5cm deep. Press the pastry evenly over the base and sides, trim the top edge neatly and chill for $^1/_2$ - 1hour.
3. Finely chop or mince the bacon and onion and set aside. Finely slice or grate the cheese and the apple onto two seperate plates.
4. Cover the base of the pastry case with one third of the apple, season lightly, then one third of the cheese and one third of the bacon and on-ion, sprinkle with mixed herbs. Repeat the layers twice almost filling the case.
5. Mash the potato adding a little milk to make it creamy and season, spread over the pie.
6. Brush with melted butter and bake for $1^1/_4$ hours or until cooked.
7. Serve hot or leave in tin until cold then unmould and serve like pork pie with chutneys and salad.

Jimmys Pork and Apple Pie
(Serves 8)

A marble pastry board improves both your bread and pastry making

PASTRY : 12 oz/350g white plain flour
Pinch of salt • 8oz/225g butter, diced • 2 egg yolks • Beaten egg to glaze

FILLING: 5 level tbsp/75ml wholemeal flour
1 pint/600ml light stock • 1 level tbsp/15ml ground coriander
5 fl.oz/150ml dry white wine • 1 level tsp/5ml ground paprika
2 level tsp/10ml dried sage • salt & pepper • 1 lb/450g leeks
$2^1/_2$ lb/1.1kg pork fillet • 1 lb/450g Bramleys peeled and cored
6oz/175g rindless streaky bacon • 4 tbsp/60ml olive oil
2 oz/50g spring onions chopped

1. Pre-heat oven to 325° F/170° C/mark 3
2. For the filling, mix together the flour, coriander, paprika and seasoning. Cut the pork into 1"/2.5 cm pieces and toss the meat in seasoned flour. Cut bacon into small pieces.
3. Heat a heavy based casserole and add the oil, add the bacon and fry gently until golden, remove with a slotted spoon.
4. Brown the pork in batches making sure it is sufficiently cooked, add a little more oil if it starts to stick to the pan. Return all the pork to the casserole with any remaining flour, add the bacon, stock, wine and sage and bring to the boil, place in the oven for 45 minutes.
5. Trim, rinse, drain and slice the leeks and spring onions into $^1/_2$"/1cm pieces. Peel quarter core and thickly slice the apples. Add the leeks and apples to the casserole, re-cover and bake for another 45 minutes or until the meat is tender. Adjust seasoning, cool completely and strain the juices from the cooked meat into a bowl.
6. Make the pastry, sift the flour and salt into a large bowl add the diced butter and rub into the flour until the mixture resembles fine breadcrumbs. Bind to a firm dough with the egg yolks beaten together with 3 tbsps/45ml of water. Very lightly knead, wrap in cling film and chill for 1 hr.
7. Without over-working thickly roll out just three quarters of the pastry to a round of approximately 15"/38cm diameter and use it to line a 8"/20cm spring release cake tin, take care not to split the pastry or the meat juices will run out of the pie.
8. Carefully spoon the mixture into the prepared tin and pour over 5 fl oz/150ml meat juices. Place the remaining meat juices in a saucepan ready to reheat when required.
9. Roll out the remaining pastry for the top of the pie and pinch the edges well to seal. Trim off any excess pastry and decorate the pie. Make a small hole in the centre for the steam to escape and brush with beaten egg and chill for 30 minutes. Preheat the oven to 200° C/400° F/Mark 6
10. Reglaze pie, stand tin on an edged baking tray and bake for 1 hr covering with foil to prevent over browning. Cool for 10 minutes and carefully remove tin side. Leave pie on tin base, place on an edged dish and serve with the remaining hot meat juices.

Commons Pie
(Serves 4)

1lb/450g lean lamb, cooked and sliced
1lb/450g onions, thinly sliced
1lb/450g Howgate apples, thinly sliced • 2oz/50g butter
pinch of rosemary • pinch of oregano
$^1/_2$ pint/300ml rich gravy • $^1/_2$-$^3/_4$lb/300g potatoes, diced
$^1/_2$-$^3/_4$lb/300g swede, diced • salt and pepper.

1. Pre-heat the oven to 375°F/190°/Gas 5. Put the onions and apples in a pan and cover with water. Boil for 5 minutes, drain well.
2. Meanwhile boil the swede for 10 minutes, then add the potato and cook until both are soft.
3. Drain well and mash together until smooth.
4. Grease an ovenproof dish with butter, place layers of lamb, onion and apple in the dish, seasoning and sprinkling each layer with rosemary and oregano.
5. Pour in the gravy and top with the mashed potato and swede mixture.
6. Dot the top with butter and bake uncovered for $^3/_4$ - 1 hour.

Chicken and Sweetcorn Plait
(Serves 6)

12oz/350g puff pastry • 8oz/225g cooked chicken cut into strips
6 rashers of smoked bacon diced • 1 stick of celery, sliced finely
4oz/100g can of sweetcorn • 2 Greensleeves apples, cored and diced
1 tbsp/15ml herbs de Provence • 1tbsp/15ml whole grain mustard
1 egg beaten with a little salt and water

salt and freshly round black pepper • $^1/_2$pt/300ml thick white sauce

1. Pre-heat the oven to 400°F/200°C/mark 6
2. In a heavy based pan sauté the bacon, celery and apples for 3 minutes add the herbs and season.
3. In a mixing bowl combine the chicken, mustard, corn and white sauce and add the bacon mixture.
4. Roll out the pastry into a rectangle approximately 9"/22.5cm x12"/30cm and lay it onto a baking sheet. Using the back of a knife mark the pastry into 3 equal lengthwise panels.
5. Spoon the chicken mixture onto the centre panel. Cut $^1/_2$"/1cm strips on a slant down the side panels and cross the strips over the chicken filling to form a plait.
6. Brush the plait with the egg glaze and bake for 30-35 minutes until golden brown.
7. Serve with crisp green salad or stir fry vegetables.

As an alternative filling use the Apple and Vegetable ingredients overleaf

Apple & Vegetable Plait

4oz/100g courgettes, diced
4oz/100g leeks cut into $^1/_2$"/1cm pieces
2oz/50g celery, diced
2oz/50g button mushrooms, quartered
1 small Bramley apple, diced
1 small Cox apple, diced
2oz/50g mild goats cheese, diced
2oz/50g Roquefort cheese, diced
$^1/_2$ bunch spring onions, chopped
1oz/25g chopped walnuts
1 tbsp/15ml freshly chopped parsley
1oz/25g white bread crumbs
2 garlic cloves
2oz/50g butter

1. Pre-heat oven to 400°F/200°C/mark 6
2. In a heavy based pan melt the butter and add the crushed garlic, saute the courgettes, leeks and celery for approximately 4 mins, then add the button mushrooms and continue stirring until all vegetables are lightly browned, remove from the heat, leave to cool.
3. Add all remaining ingredients to the cooled vegetables.
4. Roll out the pastry as above and spoon the Apple and Vegetable mixture onto the centre panel and complete as for Chicken and Sweetcorn Plait.

Seafood Pasta and Pear
(Serves 4)

Wines for cooking, if you can't drink it don't cook with it

1lb/450g tagliatelli • 1oz/25g butter • 1 medium onion finely chopped
1 Conference pear finely chopped • 1 tin/375g plum tomatoes
1 tsp/5ml dried basil • 1 tsp/5ml oregano • 2fl oz/50ml dry red wine
1 tsp/5ml tomato puree • 1lb/450g firm white fish • 2oz/50g prawns
salt and freshly ground black pepper • freshly grated Parmesan
freshly chopped parsley

1. Skin fish, remove any bones and cut into chunks.
2. Melt the butter in a heavy based pan and cook the onion and pear until soft. Add the tomatoes, wine, puree and herbs and bring to the boil. Boil until sauce thickens. Stir in the fish and prawns. Season and simmer for 7 to 8 minutes.
3. Cook the tagliatelli, drain and rinse with boiling water.
4. Pile into a serving dish and pour over the sauce, garnish with freshly grated Parmesan and parsley.

Mackerel with Gooseberry Sauce
(Serves 4)

Fresh fish have eyes that are clean bulging and shiny and gills that are red and clean looking

4 mackerel fillets
$^1/_2$ pt/300ml young green gooseberries
$^1/_4$ pt/150ml water
1oz/25g butter melted • 1oz/25g golden caster sugar
salt and freshly ground black pepper • pinch of ground nutmeg
1 tbsp/15ml sorrel or spinach leaves

1. Wash and finely chop the sorrel or baby spinach leaves, place in a pan with a little water and cook for 1 minute.
2. Pre-heat grill. Place the gooseberries into a heavy based pan with the water and heat until tender and mushy. Drain and sieve them.
3. Butter the grill pan and put in the mackerel skin side up, brush with a little melted butter and grill under a medium heat until cooked.
4. Add the sorrel leaves, remaining melted butter, sugar and salt, pepper and nutmeg to the gooseberries re-heat and serve with the mackerel.

Crispin Fish Kebabs
(Serves 2 as main course - 4 as starter)

Remember marinades need time !

1lb/450g Gurnard or other firm white fish
2 Crispin apples
1 small red pepper
1 small green pepper
16 prawns
4 tbsp/60ml olive oil
Juice of 1 large lemon
2 tsp/10ml fresh thyme
2 tsp/10ml fresh marjoram
salt and freshly ground black pepper

1. Skin and bone the fish and dice into 1" cubes
2. Core and peel the apples, cut into 1" cubes and drench in half the lemon juice.
3. Cut the peppers into 1" cubes and thread fish, peppers, prawns and apple onto 4 skewers
4. Mix the marinade - put the oil, remaining lemon juice, herbs and seasoning into a screw top jar and shake well. Pour over the kebabs and leave in a cool place for 2 hours. Pre-heat grill on a medium setting and grill the kebabs for 10-15 minutes turning occasionally. Serve hot with warmed pitta bread and a fresh green salad.

Crispin Pork Kebabs
(Serves 2)

8oz/225g pork fillet cubed
1 Crispin apple
1 small green pepper
1 small onion
2 tomatoes
4oz/100g mushrooms
2 tbsp/30ml dark soy sauce
2 tbsp/30ml clear honey
1 tsp/5ml ground ginger
2 tbsp/30ml lemon juice
freshly ground black pepper

When making green salads, wash the greens and roll them in a clean terry towel, refrigerate the towel until serving - the lettuce will be crisp and dry

1. Mix the marinade, put the dark soy sauce, clear honey, ground ginger, lemon juice and freshly ground black pepper into a screw top jar and shake well. Pour over the pork cubes and marinate for 4 hours before cooking. Pre-heat grill on a medium setting.
2. Cube the pepper, apple, onion, tomato and mushrooms and thread onto 2 skewers with the pork and grill for 20 minutes turning occasionally. Serve hot with warmed pitta bread and a fresh green salad.

Hedgerow Kebabs with Bramble Sauce
(Serves 4)

4 chicken breasts - boned
2 tbsp/30ml chopped fresh rosemary
Salt & black pepper
Sauce
7oz/200g blackberries
4 tbsp/60ml sweet white wine
2 tbsp/30ml redcurrant jelly
Pinch grated nutmeg
Sprigs of rosemary and whole blackberries

1. Simmer the blackberries and wine in a pan until soft, about 10 minutes.
2. Press through a sieve, return to the pan with the jelly then bring to the boil. Boil uncovered to reduce by one third.
3. Preheat the grill. Cut the chicken into 1"/2.5cm pieces and thread the meat onto 8 metal or wooden skewers.
4. Sprinkle with rosemary and seasoning and cook for 8-10 minutes until golden and evenly cooked.
5. Spoon a little bramble sauce onto each plate and place a chicken skewer on top, sprinkle with nutmeg and serve hot. Garnish with rosemary and whole blackberries.

Puddings

Raspberry Rang
(Serves 6)

6oz/175g plain flour
3oz/75g butter
1oz/25g sugar
1 egg, size 3 beaten
3 egg whites (size 3)
5oz/125g caster sugar
1 tsp/5ml white wine vinegar
1 tsp/5ml cornflour
1lb/450g fresh Raspberries

1. Pre-heat the oven to 400°F/200°C/mark 6.
2. Sift the flour into a bowl and rub in the butter until the mixture resembles fine breadcrumbs. Stir in the sugar, add the egg and enough cold water to make a soft but not sticky dough.
3. Wrap in cling film and chill for 30 minutes.
4. Roll out the pastry and use to line an 8"/20 cm greased, round, deep, fluted flan tin and bake blind. Leave to cool.
5. Place the egg whites in a clean grease free mixing bowl, and whisk until the egg whites are holding stiff peaks.
6. Gradually whisk in the caster sugar, a tbsp/15ml at a time, until the mixture turns thick and glossy. Ensure that the mixture is whisked stiff again after each addition of the sugar, then fold in the wine vinegar and cornflour.
7. Place the raspberries into the pastry case and cover with the meringue mixture and bake for 20-30 minutes until the meringue is browned.

Summer Pavlova

(Serves 6-8)

5 egg whites (size 3)
10oz/300g caster sugar
2 tsp/10ml white wine vinegar
2 tsp/10ml cornflour

FILLING:
8fl oz/250ml double cream
1 tbsp/15ml caster sugar
1 tbsp/15ml creme de cassis
12oz/350g Greek strained yogurt
6oz/175g raspberries
4oz/100g strawberries, halved
4oz/100g blueberries

1. Pre-heat oven to 300°F/150°C/Gas 2. Lightly grease two baking sheets and line with non stick baking paper, draw an 8"/20cm diameter circle on the paper covering one baking sheet and a 7"/18cm diameter circle on the other.
2. Place the egg whites in a mixing bowl, and whisk until they are holding stiff peaks
3. Gradually whisk in the caster sugar, a tbsp/15ml at a time, until the mixture turns thick and glossy. Ensure that the mixture is whisked stiff again after each addition of sugar, then fold in the wine vinegar and cornflour.
4. Swirl three-quarters of the meringue over the large circle, then spoon the rest around the smaller circle. Bake for 5 minutes then reduce the oven temperature to 250°F/120°C/mark $^1/_2$, bake for 50-55 minutes until crisp on the outside.
5. Transfer the meringues to a wire rack to cool, then carefully peel away the non-stick paper. Leave to cool completely.
6. Make the filling: whip the cream with the sugar until it just holds its shape, then fold in the creme de cassis and yogurt. Sandwich the meringues with most of the cream and fruit, then pile the rest on top. Decorate with a few extra berries. Serve at once.

Greengage and Ginger Meringues
(Serves 4)

1lb/450g greengages, halved and stoned
1 tbsp/15ml golden caster sugar
2 tbsp/30ml ginger syrup-from a jar of preserved ginger
$^1/_2$ pt/300ml double cream • 2 pieces of preserved stem ginger.

MERINGUES
1 egg white size 3 • 2oz/50g golden caster sugar
1oz/25g blanched almonds, finely chopped
slices of preserved stem ginger to decorate

1. Place the greengages in a heavy based pan with a little water and cook uncovered for 15 to 20 minutes until soft.
2. Drain off any excess liquid and leave the greengages to cool slightly, then puree in a blender with the sugar and ginger syrup. Set aside until cold. Chop 1 piece of stem ginger.
3. Whip the cream until it forms soft peaks, fold in the greengage puree and the chopped stem ginger. Spoon the cream mixture into individual serving dishes and refrigerate until ready to serve.
4. Pre-heat oven to 250°F/130°C/mark 1/2 and line a baking tray with non-stick baking paper
5. In a small bowl whisk the egg white until stiff and gradually whisk in the sugar until the mixture is thick and glossy, then with a metal spoon gently fold in the almonds.
6. Using a piping bag fitted with a $^1/_2$"/1.25 cm plain nozzle, pipe 12 meringues. Dry out in the oven for approx 1hr until crisp. Cool on a wire rack.
7. Decorate the creams with slices of the remaining preserved ginger and serve with the meringues.

Blueberry Syllabub
(Serves 4-6)

4 fl oz/120ml dry sherry
4 tbsp/60ml brandy
4 tbsp/60ml lemon juice
3 oz /75g golden caster sugar
12 fl oz/360ml double cream
8 oz/225g blueberries

1. Mix together the sherry, brandy, lemon juice and sugar until the sugar has dissolved.
2. Stir in the cream and beat with an electric or balloon whisk until the mixture forms soft peaks. Place a few blueberries in the base of 4 or 6 stemmed glasses, spoon in a layer of syllabub and repeat the layers to the top of the glass allowing a few blueberries to be left over.
3. Decorate with a few blueberries and a lemon wedge.

Rhubarb and Elderflower Syllabub
(Serves 4)

6 Rhubarb stems
9 tbsp/135ml elderflower wine
4oz/100g golden caster sugar
2 tsp/10ml ground ginger
2 tsp/10ml arrowroot
$^1/_2$ pt/300ml double cream
Lemon juice
Brandy

1. Cut the rhubarb into pieces and place in a heavy based pan with 3 tbsp/45ml of the wine, 2oz/50g of the sugar and the ginger and simmer until the fruit is tender.
2. Mix the arrowroot with a little cold water and stir into the rhubarb. Heat and stir continuously until thickened and leave to cool.
3. Set aside 3 tbsp/45ml of the rhubarb and spoon the rest into serving glasses.
4. Whip the double cream and then whisk the lemon juice, brandy, and the remaining sugar and wine into the cream.
5. Spoon into the top of the glasses, decorate with the remaining rhubarb and chill before serving.

Blackcurrant Scone Pudding
(Serves 6)

1¹/₂ lb/700g blackcurrants
6oz/175g golden caster sugar
3fl oz/90ml water
1oz/25g cornflour dissolved in a little water
8oz/250g tub of mascarpone cheese

TOPPING
6oz/175g self-raising flour
1 tsp/5ml baking powder
2oz/50g demerara sugar
grated zest and juice of 1 large lemon
2oz/50g butter melted
3fl oz/90ml milk

1. Pre heat the oven to 400°F/200°C/mark 6
2. Place the blackcurrants in a heavy based pan with 4oz/100g of sugar and the water.
3. Bring to the boil, stir and add the cornflour paste. Stir well, then reduce the heat and cook for a further 3 minutes.
4. Pour into a round ovenproof dish approximately 7¹/₂"/19cm wide and 3"/7.5cm deep and leave to cool.
5. Mix the mascarpone with the remaining sugar until thoroughly blended. Then using two tablespoons, one for the mixture and one to scrape it off, drop 6 spoonfuls of the mascarpone over the blackcurrants. Do not spread the blobs together.
6. For the topping sift the flour and the baking powder into a bowl and add the sugar and lemon zest.
7. Stir in the lemon juice and melted butter, add the milk and combine very gently (it should have a dropping consistency)
8. Drop 6 spoonfuls of the scone dough over the mascarpone, don't worry if it does not cover it exactly.
9. Place in the middle of the oven and bake for approx 25 minutes until the scone topping has risen to a golden brown.
10. Cool for 5-10 minutes and serve.

Raspberry Ripple Cheesecakes
(serves 4)

BISCUIT BASE:-
3 oz /75g plain flour
$1/_2$ oz/15g cornflour
pinch salt
1 oz/25g icing sugar
2 oz/50g butter
1 egg yolk
2 drops vanilla essence

FILLING:-
7 oz/200g soft cream cheese
3 oz/75g caster sugar
2 eggs separated
4 fl oz/120ml soured cream
$1/_2$ oz/15g gelatine

RIPPLE:-
10 oz/275g raspberries (few raspberries to decorate)
4 oz/100g icing sugar
$1/_2$ tsp/2.5ml arrowroot

1. Grease 4, 4"/10cms loose bottomed tart tins. Preheat the oven to 400°F/ 200°C/Gas 6.
2. Sieve together the flours, salt and icing sugar into a bowl, chop the butter into pieces and add to the flour. Work ingredients together with your fingertips until the butter is incorporated.
3. Stir in the egg yolk and vanilla essence and mix to form a dough. Flour the work surface and roll out the pastry. Cut circles to fit the base of the tins, prick the pastry bottoms with a fork and leave to rest in the fridge for about 30 minutes. When chilled place in the oven and bake blind for 15 minutes. Leave to cool.
4. Make up the filling by beating the cheese and sugar together. Add the egg yolks and beat well. Stir in the soured cream. Place 3 tbsp/45ml water in a small bowl, sprinkle the gelatine onto the liquid. Stand the bowl over a saucepan of hot water and stir the gelatine until it has dissolved completely. Leave to cool then stir into the cheese mixture.
5. Whisk the egg whites until stiff and fold carefully into the mixture. Leave to one side.
6. Make up the fruit puree by passing the raspberries through a sieve into a bowl to get rid of the seeds. Sieve in the icing sugar and arrowroot and mix with the raspberry puree.
7. To make the ripple, spoon the puree on top of the cheese mixture and using a skewer very gently stir the puree into the mixture to form ripples. Carefully spoon the mixture into prepared tins and swirl a little puree on top. Tap the tins to level the mixture, leave to set in a fridge. When ready remove from the tins and serve decorated with fresh raspberries.

Souffled Pancakes with Blackcurrant Compote
(Serves 6-8)

3 eggs, size 3, separated • pinch of salt • $^1/_2$ pt/300ml milk • Icing sugar
2oz 50g butter • 7oz/200g plain flour • 1lb/450g blackcurrants
2-3"/5cm cinnamon stick, a few cloves • sugar

1. Make the compote by stewing the blackcurrants slowly over a low heat with the cinnamon and cloves, a little water and enough sugar to cut the sharpness. When soft remove from the heat and keep warm.
2. Beat the egg yolks, salt, milk and flour lightly. Whisk the egg whites until stiff and fold into the mixture.
3. Melt the butter in a wide frying pan, tip in the pancake mixture and roll it around. As it sets use a knife and fork to turn it and cut it into soft strips.
4. When just set tip the strips into a serving bowl and serve immediately with the compote and a shaker of icing sugar.

Steamed Victoria Pudding
(Serves 6)

2oz/50g caster sugar • 10fl oz/300ml water
$1^1/_2$ lb/675g Victoria plums, stoned and chopped

FOR THE SPONGE
4oz/100g unsalted butter, plus extra for greasing the basin
5oz/125g golden caster sugar
1 vanilla pod
2 eggs size 3 • 1 egg yolk size 3
7oz/200g self raising flour
finely grated zest and juice of $^1/_2$ lemon

1. Grease a $1^1/_2$ pt/900ml basin with butter
2. Dissolve the sugar in the water and boil for a few mins to make a syrup. Add the plums and cook very gently for 8-10 minutes.
3. Mix the butter and the sugar until very pale, add the insides of the vanilla pod and then beat in the eggs and egg yolk. Fold in the flour using a large metal spoon and add the lemon juice and zest.
4. Spoon most of the plums and syrup into the bottom of the basin and cover with the sponge mixture to come three-quarters of the way up the side. Cover with buttered foil, allowing for expansion and place in a steamer or a pan half full of hot water over a gentle heat and steam for 1 $^1/_2$ hours.
5. When cooked turn out onto a plate and spoon over the remaining hot syrupy plums.

Damson Snow
(serves 6)

2lb/900g damsons • 2 tbsp/30ml golden granulated sugar
2 egg whites • 3oz/75g golden caster sugar • a little icing sugar

1. Put the damsons into a casserole with 1 tbsp water, cover tightly and cook in a very low oven until perfectly tender.
2. Stir in the granulated sugar, cover again and leave until cold. Stone the fruit and puree in a processor or pass through a sieve.
3. Whisk the egg whites to stiff peaks, gradually incorporating the caster sugar. Fold the egg whites into the damson pulp adding a little icing sugar if too sharp.
4. Spoon the mixture into serving glasses and chill for no more than 2 hours before serving or it may separate out.

Brandied Cherries and Pears Flaumbé
(Serves 4)

3 oz/75g soft brown sugar • 5 whole cloves
$^1/_2$ pt/300ml red wine • 2 Comice or Concorde pears
grated rind of 1 lemon • 14oz/400g fresh black cherries
1 miniature bottle cherry brandy

1. Place the sugar, cloves and red wine in an oven to tableware dish. Heat gently and stir until the sugar has dissolved.
2. Peel, core and thinly slice the pears, poach in the red wine for 10 minutes or until soft and slightly transparent.
3. Add lemon rind and black cherries and cook for a further 5 minutes. Pour the cherry brandy onto the cherries, leave on the heat for 2 minutes.
4. Remove from the heat and carefully set it alight. Let the flames disappear completely then serve directly from the pan.

Strawberry Amaretti Cream
(Serves 4-6)

$^1/_4$ pt/150ml double cream • $^1/_4$ pt/150ml Greek Yogurt
1oz/25g golden caster sugar
2oz/50g Amaretti biscuits roughly crushed • 12oz/350g strawberries sliced
4 whole strawberries to decorate • 4 Amaretti biscuits to decorate

1. Whip the cream until stiff, fold in the yogurt, sugar and biscuits.
2. Using a spatula gently fold sliced strawberries into the cream.
3. Turn into a dish, decorate and serve at once.

Strawberry Delight
(Serves 4-6)

1lb/450g strawberries hulled
3fl oz/90ml fresh orange juice
5 tbsp/75ml Grand Marnier liqueur
grated rind of one lemon
$^1/_2$ pt/300ml double cream
1oz/25g sieved icing sugar

1. Put 12oz/350g of the strawberries into a bowl with the orange juice, liqueur and lemon rind and marinate for a few hours in the fridge.
2. Drain the liquid from the fruit, remove the lemon rind and reserve both.
3. Just before serving whip the cream until stiff and gently fold in the icing sugar, juice and liqueur.
4. Pile the strawberries into serving dishes and pour on the sweetened cream. Decorate with the remaining strawberries and lemon rind

Strawberry Cream Bombe
(Serves 6-8)

2lb/900g fresh strawberries
Extra strawberries to make the sauce
$^3/_4$ pt/450ml double cream

MERINGUE
2 egg whites
3oz/75g caster sugar
2oz/50g granulated sugar

1. To make the meringue, whisk the egg whites until stiff, fold in the sugar and place spoonfuls onto a baking tray lined with baking parchment paper. Cook in a very slow oven or overnight. Cool.
2. Liquidise the strawberries, whip the cream and fold into the strawberry puree and then add about 8-10 broken meringue halves.
3. Pour into a pudding basin and freeze for 4—6 hours. Before serving put it into the refrigerator for about $^1/_2$ hour and it will then turn out easily.
4. Pour over a sauce of pureed strawberries, sweetened with icing sugar.

Raspberry Bombes
(Serves 6)

4oz/100g raspberries
3oz/75g golden caster sugar
$^1/_2$ pt/300ml whipping cream
3oz/75g blackcurrants
3oz/75g redcurrants
4 tbsp/60ml creme de cassis
Black and Redcurrants to decorate

1. Puree the raspberries and sugar in a food processor or blender. Whip the cream and fold into the raspberry puree and freeze for 30 minutes. Strip and wash the black and redcurrants and mix them with the cassis and set aside.
2. Chill 6 individual bombe moulds in the freezer until very cold. Reserve 8 tbsps/120ml of the raspberry ice cream and using the back of a teaspoon spread the remainder over the base and sides of the moulds. Return the moulds and the reserved ice cream to the freezer and leave until the ice cream in the moulds has set completely firm.
3. Remove the moulds from the freezer and fill the centres with the soaked currants, reserving a few to use as decoration. Spread a little of the reserved ice cream over the top of each bombe to seal. Return the moulds to the freezer and freeze until the ice cream has set completely firm.
4. To unmould, dip each mould briefly into hot water then turn out on to individual serving plates. Decorate with the extra currants.

Raspberry Fool
(Serves 4)

1lb/450g raspberries
1oz/25g white or brown sugar to taste
$^1/_4$ pt/150ml double or whipping cream
$^1/_4$ pt/150ml thick custard
$1^1/_2$ tbsp/7.5ml creme de cassis or brandy

1. Hull the raspberries and set aside a few for decoration. Place the remaining raspberries in a pan with a little sugar and very little water, cover and simmer for 5-10 minutes or until soft.
2. Cool slightly then pass through a fine sieve making sure you remove any seeds. Puree and then blend 4tbsp/60ml of the raspberries with the creme de cassis or brandy.
3. Whip the cream until thick but not stiff. Gently and softly fold in raspberry puree, custard and cream until just blended. Don't overwhip or you'll lose the softness and frothy texture. Spoon liqueur puree into elegant glasses or sundae dishes and top with raspberry fool, reserved raspberries and serve.

Redcurrant Ice Cream
(Serves 6)

12oz/350g redcurrants
6oz/175g golden granulated sugar
2 egg whites size 3
$^1/_2$ pt/300ml double cream

1. Strip the redcurrants from their stalks, rinse and puree in a food processor. Push through a nylon sieve to remove all the pips.
2. Using a heavy based pan dissolve the sugar in 4fl oz/120ml of water, boil for about 5 minutes or until syrupy.
3. Whisk the egg whites until stiff, then gradually add the hot syrup, whisking all the time to keep the mixture stiff. Continue to whisk the mixture for about 5 minutes or until cool.
4. Whip the cream until it just holds its shape. Fold the cream and redcurrants into the egg white mixture and spoon into a shallow freezer container.
5. Freeze until firm—approximately 6 hrs. Take out and leave at cool room temperature for 15 minutes to soften before serving

Apple Crunch Ice-Cream with Fudge Sauce
(Serves 6)

3oz/75g brown breadcrumbs • 2oz/50g demerara sugar
2 tsps/10ml mixed spice
1lb/450g Cox or Katy eating apples including one Bramley
Golden caster sugar to taste • $1^1/_2$ pt/900ml double cream
Fudge sauce:
7oz/200g soft, light brown sugar • $^1/_4$ pt/150ml double cream
4oz/100g unsalted butter

1. Pre-heat oven to 375°F/190°C/mark 5
2. Mix together the breadcrumbs, demerara sugar and mixed spice and scatter on a baking tray. Bake for 10 minutes stirring occasionally. Leave to cool.
3. Core and dice the apples. Place in a heavy based pan with 2fl oz/60ml of cold water and caster sugar, simmer over a low heat until soft. Beat and then leave to cool.
4. Whip the cream, fold in the breadcrumb and apple mixtures. Pour into a rigid plastic container and freeze. Transfer to the fridge to soften then place scoops on to foil-lined trays for 30 minutes in the freezer before serving.
5. Meanwhile make the fudge sauce by mixing all the ingredients together in a pan over gentle heat. Bring to the boil, then simmer for 2 to 3 minutes until a pale caramel. Serve warm poured over the ice-cream.

Gooseberry Fool
(Serves 4-6)

2lb/900g gooseberries
6oz/175g golden caster sugar
12oz/375ml double cream
Sponge finger biscuits for serving

1. Top and tail the gooseberries and put in a saucepan with the sugar and a splash of water. Cover and simmer gently until tender.
2. Drain, reserving the juice and press through a sieve.
3. Chill the puree and juice until very cold.
4. Whip the cream in a large chilled serving bowl until the whisk forms peaks.
5. Carefully fold in the gooseberry puree and some of the juice so that the mixture is streaky and serve with sponge finger biscuits and extra sugar if required.

Gooseberry and Lime Fool
(Serves 4)

$1^1/_4$lb/550g gooseberries, topped and tailed
1 lime jelly
2 eggs, size 3 seperated
2 tbsps/30ml Double cream
golden caster sugar to taste

1. Place the gooseberries in a heavy based pan with a little water and cook until soft.
2. Add the jelly cubes and let them dissolve in the gooseberries. Sweeten to taste.
3. Liquidise the gooseberries. Beat in the egg yolks add the cream and stir these into the gooseberries. Leave until semi set.
4. Whip up the egg whites until they form soft peaks and fold into the gooseberries.
5. Place in individual serving dishes and refrigerate until set.

Tipsy Summer Pudding
(Serves 6-8)

6oz/175g gooseberries
6oz/175g redcurrants
6oz/175g blackcurrants
6oz/175g strawberries
6oz/175g blackberries
6oz/175g raspberries
3tbsp/45ml water
$^1/_8$ pt/75ml creme de cassis
$^1/_8$ pt/75ml brandy
unsliced loaf stale bread

1. Thoroughly pick over the fruit. If the strawberries are large cut them into quarters.
2. In a pan large enough to hold all the fruit bring the water, brandy and creme de cassis to the boil.
3. Add the gooseberries to the pan and cook them until their skins burst.
4. Add the blackberries, black and red currants and simmer gently for 5 minutes until soft.
5. Lastly, add the strawberries and raspberries, mix well then take off the heat and leave to cool.
6. Slice the bread thinly and cut off the crusts, put aside 3 rounds for the top, middle and bottom of a 2pt/1200ml basin. Cut the remaining bread into fingers to fill all the gaps and sides.
7. Place a round into the bottom of the basin and use the fingers to line the sides. Fill with the mixture packing it well to half way up and add another round before pouring in the remaining fruit, finishing with the last round of bread. Make sure the liquid has soaked the bread thoroughly.
8. Stand your basin on a large plate to catch any leakage and place another plate just inside the pudding basin and then put a weight on top and leave in the fridge for at least 24 hours.

Plain sponge cake can be used instead of bread if preferred.

Fruit Brulee
(Serves 4)

1lb/450g mixed fruit
sugar to taste
1 tbsp/15ml cornflour
2 tbsp/30ml water
$^1/_2$ pt/300ml double cream
$^1/_2$ pt/300ml thick and creamy yogurt
4oz/100g soft brown sugar
7"/17.5cm ovenproof souffle dish

Sunberries, Strawberries, peaches, plums or gages are a good combination

1. Warm the fruit until the juices flow, add the sugar to taste. Mix the cornflour with water and add to the fruit, bring to the boil and heat until thickened, take off heat immediately, place in a dish and leave to cool.
2. Beat the cream until peaks form and fold in the yogurt. Put onto the cold fruit. Sprinkle on the brown sugar, place under a hot grill, wait for a few minutes until the sugar is dark, when cool place in a fridge and leave overnight before serving.

Redcurrants in Port
(Serves 4)

2lb/900g redcurrants
2-4oz/50-100g golden granulated sugar to taste
7fl oz/200ml of port
Slices of galia melon

1. Strip the redcurrants from their stalks, rinse and drain.
2. Dissolve the sugar in the port with 5fl oz/150ml of water. Boil for 2 minutes. Stir in the redcurrants and immediately pour out into a heatproof bowl to cool.
3. Cover the redcurrants and chill before serving. Accompany with thick slices of galia melon.

Rhu-berry Jelly
(Serves 4-6)

Use either late summer rhubarb or Frozen blackberries to make this delicious jelly—as this jelly is a combination of spring and autumn

1 lb/450g fresh rhubarb
8oz/225g blackberries
1 tsp/5ml ground nutmeg
5oz/125g packet blackcurrant jelly
1 tbsp/15ml toasted flaked almonds, to decorate
Almond biscuits to serve

1. Wash, trim and cut the rhubarb into even sized chunks. Place the rhubarb blackberries and nutmeg into a large saucepan with $^1/_4$ pint/150ml water. Simmer for ten minutes or until tender.
2. Puree the fruit. Dissolve the jelly in $^3/_4$ pt boiling water, stir into rhubarb and blackberry puree. Pour the mixture into serving dishes. Stand dishes on a flat surface in the fridge for up to 3 hours to give a soft set.
3. When set remove from the fridge and decorate with the toasted almonds. Serve with almond biscuits.

Fruity Bread Pudding
(Serves 4-6)

6oz/175g Raspberry & Apple or Blackberry & Apple (Bramley Apples)
9 medium slices white bread
$1^1/_2$ oz/37.5g softened butter
6 egg yolks
$7^1/_2$ fl oz/225ml milk
$7^1/_2$ oz/225ml double cream
vanilla essence or 1 vanilla pod
4oz/100g golden caster sugar

1. Pre-heat oven to 350°F/175°C/mark 4
2. Partially cook the Apple and as it cools add the raspberries/blackberries. Set aside
3. Grease a 2-3pt flat ovenproof dish and butter the bread
4. Whisk the egg yolks and caster sugar together in a bowl
5. Place the milk and cream in a pan with the vanilla pod and slowly bring to simmer, remove the pod and pour slowly on to the egg yolks stirring constantly
6. Place the cooled fruit at the bottom of the dish and arrange the slices of bread on top, sealing the edges as well as possible.
7. Pour over the warm custard and bake for 45 minutes - 1 hour or until the top is crisp and golden. Sprinkle with golden caster sugar and serve.

Mulled Orchard Fruits
(Serves 4)

2 tbsp/30ml clear honey • 5 drops oil of cinnamon
1 strip of orange zest, shredded
1 tsp/5ml mixed peppercorns, lightly crushed
8oz/225g Gala apples, cored and sliced
8oz/225g William or Comice pears peeled, cored and sliced
8oz/225g Czar, Monarch or Cropper plums stoned and sliced
$^1/_2$ pt/300ml dry cider

1. Put the honey, cinnamon, shredded orange zest and mixed pepper-corns into a heavy-based pan
2. Gently heat so the honey melts and the ingredients are cooked lightly
3. Add the fruits and stir so they are all coated with the flavoured honey
4. Add the cider and cook gently until the fruits are cooked - approximately 15 minutes
5. Serve warm with vanilla ice-cream

Plummy Apple Crumble
(Serves 6-8)

FILLING:-
1lb/450g Prolific plums halved and stoned
$1^1/_2$ lb/675g Grenadier apples peeled quartered cored and sliced
2oz /50g golden caster sugar
1tsp/5ml ground mixed spice

TOPPING:-
4oz/100g plain flour
4oz/100g butter
4oz/100g light soft brown sugar
3oz/75g rolled oats
2oz/50g pecan or walnut halves, chopped and toasted
freshly grated nutmeg (optional)

1. Pre-heat the oven to 190°c/375°F/mark 5.
2. Cook the apples with the sugar and spice in a covered pan over a low heat for 15 minutes, stir in the plums and transfer to a pie dish.
3. To make the crumble - sift the flour into a bowl and rub in the butter, stir in the brown sugar rolled oats and nuts. Flavour with grated nutmeg.
4. Spoon the crumble mixture on top of the berries and press down lightly. Bake for about 30-35 minutes or until golden brown. Serve warm or cold with custard or cream.

Apple Pond Pudding
(Serves 6)

PASTRY
12 oz/350g self raising flour
pinch salt
6 oz/175g shredded suet
$^1/_2$ tsp/2.5ml ground cinnamon • grated rind of 1 lemon
1 small lemon, well scrubbed
4oz/100g demerara sugar
4oz/100g butter, cubed
12oz/350g Newton Wonder cooking apples, cored and sliced

1. Sift the flour and salt into a large mixing bowl, stir in the suet, cinnamon and rind, gradually mix in the cold water until you have formed a soft but not too sticky dough.
2. Knead the dough very lightly on a floured work surface and roll out into a large round, about $^1/_4$"/.5cm thick. Cut a quarter sized wedge from the dough and set it aside for the lid.
3. Shape the remaining three-quarters of the dough into a cone and then ease it into a $2^1/_2$pt/1.5lt pudding basin leaving an overhang. Press into place.
4. Prick the lemon all over with a skewer.
5. Mix together the demerara sugar and butter, layer the apple slices and butter mixture in the basin placing the lemon in the centre as you go.
6. Re-roll the remaining dough into a round for the lid, brush the edges with water and place in position. Press the edges together to seal completely. Trim away excess.
7. Cover the pudding basin with buttered greaseproof paper and foil. Make a wide pleat in the middle of both to allow for expansion during cooking. Tie securely with string leaving enough for a handle.
8. Steam the pudding for $3^1/_2$ - 4 hrs, topping up the pan regularly with boiling water to avoid it boiling dry.
9. Turn out the pudding and serve immediately with pouring cream or custard.

Apricot Apples
(Serves 4)

4 medium Newton Wonder cooking apples
3oz/75g natural dried, no-soak apricots, chopped
3oz/75g soft light brown sugar • a pinch of ground coriander
$^1/_4$ pt/150ml apple juice • 2oz/50g butter

1. Pre-heat oven to 180°C/350°F/mark 4.
2. Core the apples and cut a shallow slit around the middle of each one and place in a greased, shallow ovenproof dish.
3. Mix together the apricots, sugar and coriander and pack tightly into the apple cavities. Scatter the remaining filling around the apples. Pour on the apple juice and dot the apples with pieces of the butter.
4. Place uncovered in the oven for approx 40 minutes or until they are just tender.

Under Pressure Plum Pudding
To 10lb pressure or setting 2 (medium)
10 mins at 15lb pressure or setting 3 (high)

1lb/450g Czar or Cropper plums, halved and stoned
2 oz/50g golden caster sugar • 3 oz/75g butter • lemon juice
4 oz/100g wholemeal breadcrumbs • 4 oz/100g demerara sugar

1. Place the plums in a greased 1pt/600ml ovenproof souffle dish. Sprinkle with caster sugar and cover with foil, tied down securely. Put $^1/_2$ pt/300ml water with a drop of lemon juice into the cooker and place the dish on the trivet.
2. Close cooker and bring to 10lb pressure or setting 2 (medium) then take off heat. Release steam slowly, strain the plums, reserving the juice so that only the fruit is used. Wash the dish and grease lightly.
3. Melt 2 oz/50g butter in a frying pan and fry the breadcrumbs until golden. Remove the crumbs from the pan and mix with half the demerara sugar. Place a layer of plums in the dish and sprinkle with a layer of crumb mixture. Build up in layers finishing with a crumb layer.
4. Cover the dish with greased foil, tied down well with string. Put 1pt/600ml fresh water into the cooker plus a drop of lemon juice, the trivet and stand the pudding on the base. Close the cooker. Bring to 15lb pressure or setting 3 (high) and cook for 10 minutes. Release steam slowly.
5. Dot the top of the pudding with remaining butter and sprinkle with the rest of the sugar. Brown under a hot grill for approximately 3 minutes.

Plum Charlotte
(Serves 4-6)

4oz/100g Butter
6oz/175g fairly coarse breadcrumbs
3oz/75g soft brown sugar
1lb/450g ripe purple Pershore plums, halved and stoned

1. Pre heat oven to 320°F/160°C/mark 3.
2. Heat the butter in a large, heavy-based, frying pan and cook the breadcrumbs until they are golden brown and crisp.
3. Tip the breadcrumbs into a basin and mix with the sugar.
4. Put one third of the crumbs into a basin cover with half of the plums.
5. Cover with the second third of crumbs, the rest of the filling and a final layer of crumbs.
6. Bake in the centre of the oven for approximately 45-50 minutes.

For a different flavour, use yellow egg plums. Halve and stone the plums, place in a dish and sprinkle with brown sugar. Leave overnight, and then use as above.

Breads, Cakes
and
Pastries

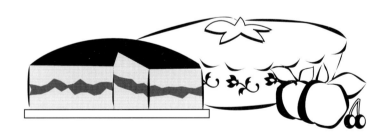

Grandma's Raspberry Pie
(Serves 6)

6$\frac{1}{2}$ oz/190g plain flour
4oz/100g butter
3 pinches of salt
1tbsp/15ml of lemon juice
1lb/450g raspberries
2tbsp/30ml water
4oz/100g golden caster sugar and extra sugar for dusting
1 egg white lightly beaten
$\frac{1}{2}$ pt/10 fl oz whipping cream
2-3 egg yolks

1. Put the flour in a bowl with the salt. Take a block of butter from the fridge and fold back paper, grate the butter coarsely into kitchen scales.
2. Mix quickly into the flour using a knife and bind with the lemon juice and iced water.
3. Wrap and chill dough for 30 minutes—1 hour. Pre-heat oven to 375°F/190°C/mark 5.
4. Roll out half the pastry and use to line a round 8"/20cm pie plate.
5. Layer the raspberries and sugar and mound up above the level of the rim of the plate
6. Cover with the remaining pastry, make a hole in the top with the end of a small kitchen funnel.
7. Brush the pie with lightly beaten egg white and sprinkle with a little sugar and bake until the pastry is pale and cooked.
8. Warm the cream to boiling point whisk into the yolks and pour slowly through the central hole down the funnel while the pie is still hot. It may not all fit, so be careful. Return pie to the oven for 10 minutes. Any cream and egg remaining can be sweetened and gently heated to form a little extra custard.

Ye Olde Apple Pie
(serves 6-8)

10oz/275g plain flour
6oz/175g hard butter
1$^1/_2$ tbsp/22.5ml lemon juice
2 tbsp/30ml iced water
4 pinches of salt
1$^1/_2$-2lbs/675-900g Bramley Apples
large knob butter
soft brown sugar to taste
pinch cinammon or nutmeg (optional)
milk
lemon juice

1. Pre-heat oven to 400°F/200°C/mark 6
2. Put the flour & salt into a bowl and grate in the butter, mix quickly with a knife and bind with the lemon juice and iced water. Wrap and chill for 30 minutes
3. Peel, core and slice the apples and partially cook with a knob of butter, adding the sugar to taste and spices if desired. Cool.
4. Roll out half the pastry to fit a 8"/20cm deep pie dish and fill with the cooked apple mixture.
5. Roll out the remaining pastry and cover the pie - press the edges together to seal and trim and flute the edges, cut a hole in the centre of the pie, brush the top with milk. Cook for 15 minutes then lower heat to Gas 5/375°F/190°C and bake for a further 20 minutes until the pastry is golden. Sprinkle with caster sugar and serve with custard, ice cream or cream.

Lazy Days Flan
(Serves 6)

8oz/225g plain flour
Finely grated rind of 1 orange
4oz/100g unsalted butter
4 tbsp/60ml orange juice
13fl oz/400ml creme fraiche
2 eggs size 3 beaten
1 tbsp/15ml golden caster sugar
1 tsp/5ml vanilla essence
Pinch grated nutmeg
1lb/450g mixed summer fruit
4 tbsp/60ml Cointreau
Icing sugar to decorate

Try a selection of Loganberries or Tayberries with Strawberries and Peaches

1. Preheat oven to 440°F/220°C/mark 6
2. Sift flour into a bowl and stir in the orange rind and rub in the butter.
3. Stir in orange juice and mix to form a light dough. Roll out onto a highly floured surface and line a 10"/25cm flan dish.
4. Bake flan case blind for 20 minutes.
5. Beat together the creme fraiche, eggs, caster sugar, vanilla essence and nutmeg. Pour into the flan case reduce oven temperature to 180°C/350°F/gas 5 and cook for a further 30 minutes and leave to cool.
6. Toss the summer fruits in the contreau and put into flan, sift over a little icing sugar and serve with cream or creme fraiche.

Golden Pear Tart

(Serves 6)

6oz/175g plain flour
3oz/75g butter
1oz/25g sugar
1 egg, size 3 beaten

FILLING
4oz/100g butter softened
4oz/100g soft light brown sugar
2 eggs size 3 beaten
1 tbsp/15ml brandy
4oz/100g ground almonds
4 drops almond essence
1 tbsp/15ml self-raising flour

TOPPING
3 Comice pears
2 tsp/10ml golden caster sugar
3 tbsp/45ml sieved apricot jam

1. Pre-heat oven 400°F/200°c/mark 6.
2. Sift the flour into a bowl, rub in the butter until the mixture resembles fine breadcrumbs. Stir in the sugar, add the egg and enough cold water to make a soft but not sticky dough.
3. Wrap in cling film and chill for 30 minutes
4. Roll out the pastry and use to line an 8"/20cm round, deep, fluted flan tin and bake blind.
5. Meanwhile make the filling, cream the butter and sugar until pale and light.
6. Gradually beat in the eggs, beating well after each addition.
7. Fold in the remaining ingredients and then spoon the mixture into the cooked pastry case and spread evenly.
8. Peel and halve the pears, scoop out the cores and slice across widthways. Fan the pears into the almond cream retaining the shape of each pear half and bake for 10-15 minutes.
9. Reduce the oven to 350°F/180°C/mark 4 and bake for a further 5 to 10 minutes or until the almond mixture is set. Sprinkle with the sugar and bake for a further 20 minutes and leave to cool.
10. Remove the cooled tart from the tin and transfer to a serving plate. Heat the apricot jam and brush over to glaze the tart and serve warm or cold.

Apple Sweet Hearts
(makes 8)

8oz/225g plain flour
4oz/100g butter, cut into cubes
1oz/25g vanilla sugar
2 tsp/10ml finely grated orange rind
1 egg yolk mixed with 2 tbsp cold water

If vanilla sugar is not available, make your own by putting a vanilla pod into a jar of sugar and leave it until the required strength is reached

FILLING
1lb/450g bramley apples, peeled, cored and chopped
3 tbsp/45ml apple juice
juice of $^1/_2$ lemon
2-4 oz/50-100g vanilla sugar (to taste)
3 eggs size 3
1oz/25g butter

1. Sift the flour into a bowl and add the butter and rub in until the mixture resembles fine breadcrumbs. Stir in the vanilla sugar and orange rind, then add the egg yolk and water and mix to a firm dough. Knead briefly, wrap and chill for 1 hr.
2. Pre-heat the oven to 400°F/200°C/mark 6. Roll out the dough thinly and use to line eight heart shaped tins. Trim the edges. Prick the bases lightly with a fork and chill for 15 minutes.
3. Line the tins with greaseproof paper and baking beans and bake blind for 15 minutes, remove beans and paper and bake for a further 10 minutes or until the pastry is crisp.
4. Place the apples, apple and lemon juice in a heavy based pan and heat until reduced to a pulp, pass through a sieve and return to the pan and stir in the sugar until dissolved.
5. Beat the eggs and strain into the apple mixture. Cook over a low heat, stirring constantly until slightly thickened. Remove from the heat and beat in the butter. Spoon the mixture into pastry cases and bake for 10-15 minutes until just set and cool before serving.

Creamy Berry Tranche
(Serves 6-8)

1lb/450g puff pastry

For the creme patissiere:
8fl oz/250ml milk
8fl oz/250ml double cream
1 vanilla pod
6 egg yolks, size 3
3oz/75g golden caster sugar
1 tbsp/15ml cornflour

TOPPING
12oz/350g mixture of strawberries, blueberries, raspberries, loganberries and 1 peach
2tbsp/30ml redcurrant jelly

1. Pre heat the oven to 425°F/220°C/mark 7
2. Roll out pastry to an oblong, 12" x 8"/30x20cm. Fold in half length ways, neaten the edges with a knife and cut an oblong out of the centre leaving a 1"/2.5cm border and reserve. Open and roll out the centre piece to an oblong 12" x 8"/30 x 20cm.
3. Place this piece on a damp baking sheet. Wet the edges and open out the reserved pastry and place on top of the oblong and flute the edges. Prick the base with a fork and bake for 25 minutes. Cool on a wire rack.
4. In a heavy based pan combine milk, cream and vanilla pod. Heat the mixture until it is just about to boil. Remove from heat, cover and infuse for 10 minutes. Beat egg yolks and sugar together until pale and thick. Strain milk into egg mixture. Save the pod and use again.
5. Return the mixture to the heat. Mix the cornflour with 1 tbsp/15ml cold water. Add to the mixture and bring to the boil, whisking until the cream thickens. When the cream is thick and smooth remove from heat and cool. Spread into the pastry case.
6. Prepare the fruit to be used. Hull and halve the strawberries and thinly slice the peach. Arrange the fruit in rows on top of the cream.
7. Place the redcurrant jelly in a saucepan with 1 tbsp/15ml water, gently whisk over a low heat, until melted. While still warm brush lightly over the fruit.

Harvest Slice
(Serves 6)

12oz/350g rich shortcrust pastry
6 Concorde pears, peeled, cored and sliced
8oz/225g blackberries
2 tbsp/30ml sugar
$^1/_2$ tsp/2.5ml cinnamon
4oz/100g unsalted butter, chopped
6oz/175g plain flour
4 tbsp/60ml soft brown sugar
4 tbsp/60ml lightly toasted sesame seeds

1. Pre-heat oven to 375°F/190°C/mark 5
2. Roll out pastry and line a Swiss roll tin, even the top edges of the pastry and prick the base.
3. In a saucepan, mix the pears, blackberries, sugar and cinnamon with 1tbsp/15ml water. Cook for 5 minutes, or until fruit is soft but still holds its shape. Cool the fruit and set aside.
4. Using a slotted spoon, put the mixture on top of the pastry base. In a bowl, rub together the butter and flour until the mixture resembles fine breadcrumbs. Add brown sugar and sesame seeds. Sprinkle over fruit and bake for 35-40 minutes. Serve hot or cold sprinkled with more sugar.

Raspberry Torte
(serves 6)

5oz/125g butter, softened • 5oz/125g golden caster sugar
5oz/125g ground almonds • 5oz/125g white self-raising flour
1 egg size 3
1tsp/5ml ground cinnamon
8oz/225g raspberries
icing sugar

1. Place the softened butter, caster sugar, ground almonds, flour and egg in a bowl with the ground cinnamon and beat well.
2. Grease and base line a $8^1/_2$"/21.5cm spring release cake tin and preheat oven to 350°F/180°C/mark 4
3. Spread half the almond mixture into the tin, using a fork to flatten lightly. Sprinkle over the raspberries then dot over the remaining almond mixture.
4. Stand the tin on a baking sheet, then bake for approx 1hour, covering lightly when well browned. The torte should feel just firm to the touch with a springy texture. Cool in the tin for approx 1hour.
5. Carefully remove from the tin and dust with cinnamon and icing sugar.

Strawberry and Raspberry Nutty Sponge
(Serves 8)

Plain and Hazelnut Sponges:
4 eggs size 3 separated
4oz/100g icing sugar
2oz/50g plain flour
1oz/25g cornflour

Repeat the ingredients to make the hazelnut sponge,
replacing the flours with 4oz/100g roasted hazelnuts,
coarsely ground.

$^3/_4$ **pt/450ml double cream whipped**
1lb/450g raspberries
1lb/450g strawberries
icing sugar to dust

1. Pre-heat oven to 350°F/180°C/mark 4.
2. Grease and line two 9$^1/_2$"/24cm loose-bottomed cake tins dusting with flour. One for the hazelnut sponge and one for the plain sponge.
3. Whisk egg yolks with icing sugar (reserve 2tbsp/30ml of icing sugar) until pale and thick.
4. Sieve the flours onto the egg yolk mixture. Fold in with a large metal spoon to keep the sponge light. For the hazelnut sponge fold in the ground hazelnuts in place of the flours. The mixture will be quite stiff.
5. Place the egg whites into a large bowl and beat until they form soft peaks. Then beat in the remaining icing sugar.
6. With a large metal spoon fold the egg whites into the mixture adding a small amount of egg white at a time.
7. Immediately pour the mixture into the cake tin and cook for approx 20 minutes for the plain cake and for approx 30-40 minutes for the hazelnut cake. If cakes are browning too quickly cover with greaseproof paper.
8. Leave in the tin for 5 minutes before turning out onto a wire rack to cool. When cold, remove the greaseproof paper and slice the cake horizontally into 2 layers.
9. Spread the plain bottom layer with half the cream, top with a hazelnut layer, spoon on all the raspberries dusted with a little icing sugar and then add a plain layer of cake and the remaining cream.
10. Top with a hazelnut layer and finish with strawberries and a dusting of icing sugar.

Toffee Apple Crumble Cake
(serves 6-8)

6oz/175g butter softened slightly
6oz/175g muscovado sugar
3 eggs, size 3, lightly beaten
6oz/175g self raising flour
1-2 tbsp/15-30ml apple juice
1 Gala apple, chopped

Mixing a tbsp/15ml of the flour with the eggs tends to stop the cake mixture curdling and gives a better texture

FOR THE CRUMBLE
1oz/25g butter, softened
2oz/50g plain flour
1 tbsp/15ml demerara sugar
1 tbsp/15ml chopped mixed nuts

FOR THE ICING
2 tbsp/30ml icing sugar
2 tsp/5ml apple juice

1. Pre-heat oven to 375°F/190°C/mark 5.
2. Grease a 2"/5cm deep 8"/20cm loose bottomed cake tin and line the base.
3. Beat together the butter and sugar until pale, gradually beat in the eggs.
4. Fold in the flour and enough apple juice to give a dropping consistency. Fold in all but 2 tbsp of the apple, spoon the mixture into the tin.
5. To make the crumble top, rub the butter into the flour, stir in the sugar and nuts and spread over the cake with the remaining apple.
6. Bake for 45-50 minutes or until a skewer inserted into the centre, comes out clean. Turn out onto a wire rack and cool.
7. Mix together the icing sugar and apple juice and drizzle over the cake. Cut into squares when set.

Braun Apple Cake
(Serves 10-12)

Use Cox or Russett apples for a change. These hold their shape.

FOR THE BASE:-
6oz/175g self raising flour
3oz/75g light soft brown sugar
3oz/75g ground almonds
$4^1/_2$ oz/115g butter
1 egg, size 3 beaten
$1^1/_2$ tsp/7.5ml lemon juice

FOR THE FILLING:-
$1^1/_2$ lbs Bramley apples
$4^1/_2$ oz/130g light soft brown sugar
$1^1/_2$ tsp/7.5ml lemon juice

FOR THE TOPPING:-
3oz/75g self raising flour
$7^1/_2$ oz/215g light soft brown sugar
1tsp/5ml ground cinnamon
3oz/75g butter

1. Preheat oven to 180°C/360°F/mark 4
2. Grease and base line a $8^1/_2$"/21.5 round loose bottomed cake tin
3. For the base sift together the flour, sugar and half the ground almonds.
4. Rub in the butter until mixture resembles fine crumbs and then mix in the egg and juice to form a dough.
5. Press the dough evenly into the tin and then cover with the remaining ground almonds
6. For the filling peel and core the apples, cut into slices and mix with the sugar and lemon juice before placing over the base.
7. For the Topping, sift together the dry ingredients then mix in the butter until crumbly and sprinkle over the apples and bake on the middle shelf of the oven for 1-$1^1/_2$ hours.
8. Leave in the tin until cold before removing then dust with a little icing sugar.

Victoria Plum Cake

12oz/350g ripe Victoria plums
4oz/100g hazelnuts
6oz/175g vanilla sugar
6oz/175g butter slightly softened
6oz/175g self raising flour
$1^1/_2$ tsp/7.5ml baking powder
1 tsp/5ml ground cinnamon
Finely grated zest of 2 oranges
3 eggs, size 3

Have your eggs at room temperature and they will blend much more easily

1. Skin the nuts and chop each into 3-4 pieces, spread them on a baking sheet, place in oven and toast lightly as the oven heats up to 350°F/180°C/mark 4.
2. Mix the flour, baking powder, sugar, cinnamon and orange zest briefly. Add the butter and eggs, beat together.
3. Spoon half the mixture into a greased and lined 8"/20cm spring clip cake tin and bake on the hot baking sheet for 25 minutes.
4. Stone and thickly slice the plums, lay them gently on the wobbly warm cake mixture spreading right out to the edge of the tin. Spoon on the rest of cake mixture and scatter with the nuts. Bake for 1 hour, cover with greaseproof paper if the top browns too quickly.
5. Let the cooked cake rest in the tin for 15 minutes then invert onto a cooling rack.

Wensleydale Apple Cake
(Serves 4)

12oz/350g Bramley apples, peeled, cored and diced
2oz/50g golden caster sugar
3oz/75g self raising flour, sifted
$^1/_2$ tsp/2.5ml baking powder
pinch salt
1oz/25g chopped hazelnuts
2oz/50g sultanas
1 egg size 3 beaten
4 tbsp/60ml sunflower oil
6oz/175g Wensleydale cheese, thickly sliced

1. Preheat oven to 350°F/180°C/Gas 4. Lightly grease and base line a 7"/17.5cm round loose bottomed cake tin.
2. Mix together the apples, sugar, flour, baking powder, salt, hazelnuts and sultanas.
3. Combine the egg and oil and stir into the dry ingredients. Spoon half of the cake mixture into the base of the prepared tin, arrange the cheese slices on top, spoon over the remaining cake mixture and level the surface with the back of a spoon.
4. Bake for about 1 $^1/_2$ hours until firm to the touch. Leave to cool before removing from the cake tin.

Farm House Gooseberry Cake
(Serves 6 - 8)

4 oz/125g butter
4 oz/125g soft brown sugar
2 eggs, size 3, beaten
8 oz/225g plain flour
1 tsp/5ml ground mixed spice
2 tsps/10ml baking powder
3-4 tbps/45-60ml fresh milk
1 lb/450g fresh gooseberries, topped & tailed
1 tbsp/15ml light demerara sugar

A deliciously spicy and moist cake, serve for tea or as a pudding

1. Preheat oven to 325°F/160°C/mark 3
2. Grease and line a deep 7"/17.5cm round cake tin.
3. Cream the butter and sugar until pale, add the eggs a little at a time, beating well after each addition. Add the flour, spice and baking powder, mix well. Add enough milk to make a soft dropping consistency, fold in the gooseberries, spoon the mixture into tin, sprinkle with demerara sugar and bake for $1^1/_2$ hrs until well risen and firm to touch.
4. Cover if browning too quickly. Leave to cool on a wire rack.
5. Serve warm or cool with custard or cream.

Apricot and Apple Breakfast Loaf
(2lb loaf)

5oz/125g self raising flour
5oz/125g wholemeal flour
$^1/_2$ oz/15g lightly toasted sesame seeds
$^1/_2$ oz/15g poppy seeds
4oz/100g polyunsaturated margarine
10oz/275g lemon curd
3 tbsp/45ml thick natural yogurt
2oz/50g no soak dried apricots, roughly chopped
2oz/50g Worcester or Discovery apples roughly chopped
2oz/50g no soak dried figs, roughly chopped
Clear honey and lightly toasted sesame seeds to decorate

1. Pre-heat oven to 375°F/190°C/mark 5
2. Grease and line a 2lb/900g loaf tin.
3. In a large bowl, beat together all of the ingredients except the fruit. Add the fruit carefully.
4. Spoon the mixture in to the lined tin and level out with the back of a spoon.
5. Place in a preheated oven and bake for 50 minutes to 1hr until risen and a skewer comes out clean.
6. Remove from the oven and cool in the tin for a few minutes,then turn out on to a wire rack and peel off paper.
7. Mix some clear honey with some toasted sesame seeds and brush over the top of the loaf.

Golden Gage and Vanilla Bread
(Serves 8)

1$^1/_4$ lbs/575g Golden Gage or Excalibur plums
$^1/_2$ oz/13g melted butter
2$^1/_2$ tbsp/37ml vanilla sugar

BREAD DOUGH:
8oz/225g strong white bread flour
$^1/_2$ packet easy blend yeast
1$^1/_2$ tsp/7.5ml vanilla sugar
zest of 1 lemon
$^1/_4$ pt/150 mls warmed milk
1oz/25g diced butter

A slow rise in a cool place is best for dough

1. Pre-heat oven to 485°F/250°C/mark 9$^1/_2$.
2. Mix and knead the dough ingredients, when smooth and elastic cover and leave it in a cool place until it has doubled in size.
3. Butter a Swiss roll tin. Knock back the puffed up dough and roll it out to fit the tin and leave the dough to prove in a warm place for 30-40 minutes then bake it for 7 minutes. Meanwhile halve and stone greengages/plums.
4. Quickly cover the part-baked dough with the halved and stoned greengages placing them cut side up, side by side. Drizzle the $^1/_2$oz/13g of melted butter over them and sprinkle with the vanilla sugar. Bake for 5 minutes. Reduce the oven temperature to 400°F/200°C/mark 6 and bake for a further 8-10minutes. Serve either warm or cold.

Preserves
and other treats

Mint Jelly
(Makes 2lbs)

4lbs/1.8kg Bramley apples
$^1/_2$ pt/300ml malt vinegar
Large bunch of mint
Granulated sugar (1lb/450g of sugar to each 1pt/600ml of juice)
A few drops of green food colouring
Finely chopped mint

1. Wash, peel and roughly chop the apples and put them into a preserving pan, along with the skins and cores. Barely cover the bottom of the pan with water and add the bunch of mint and the malt vinegar.
2. Bring to the boil and simmer until the fruit is cooked. Cool.
3. Mash down and drain overnight through a muslin bag or sieve.
4. Measure the juice, and to each 1pt/600ml add 1lb/450g of sugar. Put into a preserving pan.
5. Bring to the boil and boil rapidly until setting point is reached. Add green food colouring and chopped mint. Cool slightly and pour into warm, sterilised jars. Cover and label. Serve with lamb.

Westmoreland Chutney
(Makes 3lbs.)

$1^1/_2$ lb/675g Cropper plums, stoned and chopped
8oz/225g courgettes, peeled and chopped
4oz/100g sultanas
12oz/350g soft brown sugar
8oz/225g onions chopped
1pt/600ml malt vinegar
$^1/_2$ tsp/2.5ml ground ginger
$^1/_2$ tsp/2.5ml mustard
Salt to taste

1. Place all the ingredients in a large pan and simmer uncovered for $1^1/_2$/2 hours, until a jam-like consistency is reached.
2. Add salt to taste before poring into warm, sterilised jars. Seal and label when cold.

Sally's East Yorkshire Chutney
(Makes approx 6lbs/3kgs)

1lb/450g demerara sugar
1lb/450g raisins
2lbs/900g Bramley apples
1 $^1/_2$ lbs/675g onions
Salt
1oz/25g of ground ginger
2 pints/1200mls malt vinegar

All chutneys improve with age- keep for at least 1-2 months before using—or 12 months for perfection!

1. Mince the apple and onion.
2. Put into a preserving pan and add all the other ingredients.
3. Cook slowly for 1$^1/_2$ hours, or, until you have the colour and consistency required.
4. Pour into hot sterilised jars—seal and label when cold.

Grape and Apple Chutney
(makes 4lb)

2 lb/900g Green grapes
2 lb/900g Howgate or Grenadier apples
8oz/225g seedless raisins
1$^1/_4$ lb/575g soft brown sugar
$^1/_2$ pint/300ml cider vinegar
$^1/_4$ pint/150ml lemon juice
$^1/_2$ tsp/2.5g ground allspice
$^1/_2$ tsp/2.5g ground cloves
$^1/_2$ tsp/2.5g salt
pinch ground cinnamon
pinch paprika
grated rind $^1/_2$ lemon

A tight fitting lid to prevent drying out and shrinkage is needed— never cover with cellophane or a metal lid

1. Cut the grapes in half and discard seeds. Peel, core and chop the apples.
2. Put all ingredients into a saucepan and bring to the boil, simmer for 1 hour until soft golden brown and thick, stirring occasionally to prevent sticking.
3. Pour into hot sterilised jars. Seal and label when cold.

Rhubarb Chutney
(Makes approx 6lbs/3kgs)

3lb/1350g rhubarb
1lb/450g sultanas
3lb/1350g onions
1lb/450g brown sugar
1oz/25g curry powder
1oz/25g white pepper
$^1/_2$ oz/2.5g cayenne pepper
1 pt/600ml malt vinegar

Use firm mid-summer rhubarb rather than spring or forced rhubarb with it's high percentage of water

1. Cut the rhubarb into small pieces and remove as much of the skin as possible.
2. Mince or process the onions and sultanas and place all the ingredients in a preserving pan and heat gently for an hour keeping well stirred.
3. Remove from the heat and put into hot, sterilised jars and cover.
4. Store in a cool dry place for 3 months before use.

Cranberry and Bramley Sauce
(Serves 4-6)

4oz/100g cranberries, fresh or frozen
1oz/25g soft dark brown sugar
$^1/_2$ small orange, grated rind and juice
pinch grated nutmeg
4oz/100g mature Bramley cooking apples, cored peeled and chopped
knob of butter

Ideal with both turkey and goose

1. Place the cranberries sugar orange rind, juice and nutmeg into a pan. Cover and cook for 10 minutes.
2. Add the apples and butter and simmer for a further 15 minutes until they begin to pulp and the sauce thickens. Cool before serving.

Apple and Horseradish Sauce
(Serves 8-12)

1 lemon
3tbsp/45ml fresh horseradish, grated
3 Large Fiesta apples, cored & peeled
4 tbsp/60ml soured cream

1. Squeeze the lemon into a basin, grate in 3tbsp/45ml of fresh horseradish.
2. Add the soured cream to make a nice firm sauce.
3. Grate in the apples, stirring to prevent them discolouring. Serve with roast beef.

Apple Sauce with Sage
(serves 6)

Excellent with duck, goose or pork - it's sharp flavour cuts through these meats which just aren't the same without it

4oz/100g onion, finely chopped
knob of butter
2tsp/10ml chopped sage
1lb/450g Grenadier apples, peeled cored and thickly sliced
1tsp/5ml golden caster sugar

1. Melt the butter in a covered pan, add the onion and soften without browning too much
2. Add the sage and cook together for a few minutes, remove from heat
3. Put the sliced apples in a heavy pan with just enough water to cover the bottom, add the sugar and bring slowly to the boil, simmer gently uncovered until the apples are soft then push through a sieve into a clean pan.
4. Reheat gently adding the sage and onion mixture. Once hot remove from heat and stand covered for 10-15 minutes.

Blackberry Relish
(makes approx 6lbs/3kg)

Very good
with either
meat or fish

3lb/1350g blackberries
3 cloves
$^1/_2$ stick cinnamon
1 pt/600ml water
$^1/_4$ pt/150ml of malt vinegar
3lb/1350g sugar

1. Stew the blackberries in the water with the cinnamon and cloves until soft and well reduced.
2. Remove the spices and rub the pulp through a sieve, or strain through a jelly bag. Add the vinegar and sugar, and when the sugar has dissolved boil fast until setting point is reached, remove from the heat and bottle in hot sterilised jars.

Apple Ginger Jam
(makes approx 8lbs/4kg)

When checking whether a jam or preserve is set remember to take your pan off the heat

5lb/2.25kg sugar
4lb/2kg mixed Gala and Bramley apples
2 lemons rind and juice
1 pt/600ml water
4oz/100g preserved ginger
1 tsp/5ml ground ginger

1. Peel core and cut up the apples, tying the cores and peel in muslin.
2. Place in the preserving pan with the lemon juice, grated rind, ground ginger and water and cook until tender.
3. Remove the bag containing the peel and cores after squeezing the juice from it. Add the sugar and chopped preserved ginger, and stir until the sugar is dissolved then boil quickly until setting point is reached, remove from the heat and bottle.

Strawberry Conserve
(makes 3lbs)

2lb/900g firm strawberries
$1^1/_2$ lb/700g preserving sugar
Juice of 1 large lemon
a little butter

Using smaller sweeter strawberries gives a fuller flavour and don't wash the strawberries-wet strawberries will never make a preserve

1. Smear the butter all over the preserving pan. Hull strawberries and wipe with damp kitchen paper, layer them in the preserving pan, sprinkling them with the sugar and leave overnight.
2. Put the preserving pan over a low heat to dissolve the sugar, try to stir the pan as little as possible so as not to break up the strawberries.
3. When there are no sugar crystals left, check this by coating the back of the spoon with the juices, bring to the boil and add the lemon juice.
4. Boil rapidly for 8 minutes and check if the preserve is set. If not boil again for 3 minutes and re-test.
5. Once it's set take the pan off the heat and leave it to settle for 15 minutes
6. Bottle in sterilised jars and seal immediately, label when cold.

Mum's Golden Apple Mincemeat
(makes 5-6lb)

1 large Bramley apple
2lbs/900g Cox 's apples
1lb/450g sugar
juice & zest of 1 lemon
1tsp/5ml ground ginger
$^1/_2$tsp/2.5ml mace
2lbs/900g sultanas
2oz/50g mixed peel
3oz/75g glace cherries
2oz/50g nuts
1pt/600ml water
knob of butter
almond essence • Brandy

A very good old fashioned mincemeat with a nice tangy flavour

1. Butter the bottom of preserving pan.
2. Peel core and dice the apples and put in the pan with sultanas, mixed peel, cherries and water and cook gently.
3. Add the spices, sugar and lemon and continue cooking until consistency required. Leave to cool, add the almond essence, nuts and brandy.
4. Bottle in sterlised jars seal and label when cold.

Pears in Brandy Syrup
(Makes 2lbs/900g)

4oz/100g soft light brown sugar
$^1/_2$ pt/300ml water
finely pared rind of 1 lemon
5 drops cinnamon essence
1 tbsp/15ml whole cloves
1lb/450g Comice Pears peeled and halved
$^1/_4$ pt/150ml brandy

Choose the most perfect shaped pears for this delectable preserve which makes a wonderful desert in the wintry months

1. Put the sugar and water in a heavy based pan and boil for approx 5 minutes until syrupy.
2. Add the lemon rind and spices, then boil hard for a further 5 minutes. Remove the spices and rind and add the pears.
3. Bring back to just below the boil and then pack the pears into warm sterilised jars using a slotted spoon.
4. Add the brandy and then top up with the syrup, seal and label.

Pears in a Pickle

6 large ripe but firm William pears
1lb/450g golden caster sugar
8fl oz/250ml red wine vinegar
1tsp/5ml whole cloves
1tsp/5ml whole allspice
small piece nutmeg

Very good with ham or cold duck

1. Core, peel and cut pears into 8 slices each. Cover with water $1^1/_4$ pt/750ml. Boil rapidly for 5 minutes. Strain off and measure liquid.
2. To 1pt/600ml add sugar, vinegar and spices, pour over pears and simmer until the pieces are cooked and translucent, approx 25 minutes. Pour into a bowl and leave overnight.
3. Drain off the liquid next day into a wide shallow pan and boil rapidly to reduce it slightly.
4. Pack the pears into warm sterilised jars with the spices, pour in boiling syrup to cover. Seal while warm. Store jars for at least a month before using.

Raspberry Vinegar

2 lbs/900g raspberries
$1^3/_4$ pt/1 litre white wine vinegar
2 oz/50g golden caster sugar

1. Place the raspberries in a bowl and pour over the white wine vinegar. Leave to stand, covered, in a cool place for 2-3 days.
2. Gently press the raspberries and vinegar through a fine sieve, do not press too hard as this will make it cloudy.
3. Add the sugar and gently simmer for 5-10 minutes until sugar dissolves. Cool and pour into sterilised bottles with lids.
4. Leave in a cool dark place for up to a month before using. Use in salad dressings with a little castor sugar.

Welcoming Winter Warmer
serves 14/15

1 cinnamon stick
5 cloves
2oz/50g light muscovado sugar
2tbsp/30ml clear honey
$1^1/_2$ pts/900ml fresh orange juice
$1^1/_2$ pts/900ml unsweetened apple juice
1 orange sliced
1 Jonagored apple cored and sliced

1. Place $7^1/_2$fl oz/225ml of water into a pan and add the cinnamon stick, cloves and the sugar and bring to the boil.
2. Simmer for about 5 minutes until all the sugar has dissolved, then stir in 2 tbsp/30ml of clear honey.
3. Add the fresh orange and apple juice and heat it through gently.
4. Strain the liquid then add the orange and apple slices. Serve hot.

Bramley Fizzy
(serves 2)

2 tbsp/30ml Bramley apple puree
1tbsp/15ml lemon juice
2 scoops vanilla ice cream
$^1/_2$ pt/300ml lemonade

1. Liquidise or blend all ingredients together
2. Pour into tall glasses, add ice cubes.

Strawberry Daiquiri
(Serves 2)

2 tbsp/30ml bacardi
2 tbsp/30ml cointreau
2 tbsp/30ml lemon juice
4 ripe strawberries and some to garnish
ice

1. Pour all ingredients into a blender/liquidiser, blend then pour into serving glasses and garnish. Serve over ice.

Index

Index

A

Apple Crunch Ice-Cream with Fudge Sauce 40
Apple Ginger Jam 70
Apple and Horseradish Sauce 69
Apple Pond Pudding 46
Apple Sauce with Sage 69
Apple Sweet Hearts 54
Apple & Vegetable Plait 26
Apricot Apples 47
Apricot and Apple Breakfast Loaf 63

B

Bacon Cheese and Apple Pie 23
Berties' Bangers 20
Blackberry Relish 70
Blackcurrant Scone Pudding 34
Blueberry Syllabub 33
Braised Red Lamb 21
Bramley Fizzy 74
Bramley Fritatta 12
Bramley Lamb 21
Brandied Cherries and Pears Flambé 37
Braun Apple Cake 59
Bumbles 10

C

Celeriac and Bramley Soup 8
Chicken and Apple Korma 19
Chicken and Sweetcorn Plait 25
Commons Pie 25
Conference Soup 7

Cranberry and Bramley Sauce 68
Creamy Berry Tranche 55
Crispin Fish Kebabs 27
Crispin Pork Kebabs 28
Cheddar Spread 11

D

Damson Snow 37
Duck Breast with Pears 18

E

Emma's Pear and Watercress Soup 6

F

Farm House Gooseberry Cake 62
Festive Filler 11
Fruit Brulee 43
Fruity Bread Pudding 44
Fruity Potato Fillers 11

G

Gamekeepers Pheasant 17
Gammon with Spiced Pears 22
Glazed Duck with Cherries 19
Gloucester Spread 11
Golden Gage and Vanilla Bread 64
Golden Pear Tart 53
Gooseberry and Lime Fool 41
Gooseberry Fool 41
Grandma's Raspberry Pie 50
Grape and Apple Chutney 67
Greengage and Ginger Meringues 32

H

Harvest Slice 56
Hedgerow Kebabs with Bramble Sauce 28
Howgate and Herring Salad 9

J

Jimmys Pork and Apple Pie 24

L

Lazy Days Flan 52

M

Mackerel with Gooseberry Sauce 27
Mint Jelly 66
Mulled Orchard Fruits 45
Mum's Golden Apple Mincemeat 71

N

Nutty but Nice 11

P

Parsnip and Apple Soup 8
Pear and Stilton Salad 9
Pears in a Pickle 72
Pears in Brandy Syrup 72
Plum Charlotte 48

Plummy Apple Crumble 45
Pork Guard of Honour with Scrumpy Apple Stuffing 14
Pork with pear and hazelnut stuffing 15

R

Raspberry Bombes 39
Raspberry Fool 39
Raspberry Rang 30
Raspberry Ripple Cheesecakes 35
Raspberry Torte 56
Raspberry Vinegar 73
Redcurrant Ice Cream 40
Redcurrants in Port 43
Rhu-berry Jelly 44
Rhubarb and Elderflower Syllabub 33
Rhubarb Chutney 68

S

Sage and Spartan Liver 20
Sally's East Yorkshire Chutney 67
Sausage Topper 11
Seafood Pasta and Pear 26
Severn Bore Pork 16
Slimmers Dream 11
Souffled Pancakes with Blackcurrant Compote 36
Spicy Bramley and Pork 16
Spicy Pear Stir-Fry 14
Steamed Victoria Pudding 36
Strawberry Amaretti Cream 37
Strawberry Conserve 71
Strawberry Cream Bombe 38
Strawberry Daiquiri 74
Strawberry Delight 38
Summer Pavlova 31
Strawberry and Raspberry Nutty Sponge 57

T

Tasty Sandwich Treats 11
Tipsy Summer Pudding 42
Toffee Apple Crumble Cake 58
Tomato, Apple and Celery soup 7

U

Under Pressure Plum Pudding 47
Upton Rarebit 10

V

Victoria Plum Cake 60

W

Waldorf Salad 9
Welcoming Winter Warmer 73
Wensleydale Apple Cake 61
Westmoreland Chutney 66
Winter Bramley Chowder 6

Y

Ye Olde Apple Pie 51

No responsibility is taken for recipes that are not original or are identical to others published